Understand Shares in a Day

Third Edition

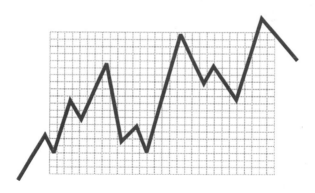

Ian Bruce
Jennie Hawthorne

TTL is an imprint of
**Take That Ltd.
P.O.Box 200,
Harrogate
HG1 2YR
ENGLAND**

email:sales@takethat.co.uk

www.takethat.co.uk

10 9 8 7 6 5 4 3 2 1

ISBN 1-873668-97-X

Contents

About the author

Ian Bruce is a successful businessman and the author of several books on finance, entrepreneurship and self-help, all of which enjoy a wide international audience. Best known for his pithy and down to earth style, he currently resides in mid-Wales.

Ian was helped by Jennie Hawthorne with the revisions and expansion of the third edition. Jennie is the author of 15 books, and is a prizewinning financial journalist who writes for national dailies, trade and consumer magazines.

Also by Ian Bruce and published by TTL...

Understand Bonds & Gilts in a Day
Understand Day Trading in a Day

... and in the same series...
Understand Derivatives in a Day
Understand Financial Risk in a Day
Understand Commodities in a Day
Understand Swaps in a Day
Understand Investment Clubs in a Day

Preface

MOST PEOPLE refer to "stocks and shares" from time to time during the course of normal conversation, but few know exactly what types of shares are available to the investing public and even fewer know how they work.

Understand Shares in a Day aims to put that right. This down-to-earth guide, which has now been expanded and revised, explains in simple terms exactly what shares are, how they work in relation to the stock market and how anyone can begin profiting from them as safely as possible. The aim is **not** specifically to encourage you to invest in shares, but to give you enough knowledge about the subject so that you can make an informed decision as to whether they would be useful in helping you to achieve your investment goals.

As a starting point, you are given a working definition for what shares represent. Then you find out about the different types of shares that are currently available, and see how they can be bought and sold. This section of the book also includes a guide to selecting a broker who is most suited to your investment needs.

Following this, we look at the role of investment and unit trusts - vehicles which can help any investor to spread the risks associated with shares whilst still leaving lots of room for potential profits. In the same vein, you will discover how it is possible to build a share portfolio to spread risk and help achieve your investment goals.

Even the most experienced financial investor will benefit from discussions about penny shares, share valuation and technical analysis.

As if all of that isn't enough to whet your appetite, this second edition includes two brand new chapters. The first, Reading Company Accounts, shows you how to read between the lines and extract valuable information from these, often tedious, documents. The second new chapter, Dealing Online, explains how you can slash your transaction costs by buying and selling via the Internet. Taking this route, you can turn more of those borderline trades into a profit.

Throughout the book you'll find examples using US dollars ($) and Pounds Sterling (£). In every case the actual currency is irrelevant and you can freely swap the symbols around as you work through the examples.

All in all, *Understand Shares in a Day* will help you decide if investing in shares is for you. Whatever your level of previous investing experience, you can be sure that the information in this indispensable title will contribute greatly to your knowledge of shares, and perhaps even to your bank account.

Introduction

JUST A FEW decades ago, share-ownership was something enjoyed by an elite and prosperous minority. To own shares in just one company - let alone a whole selection of companies - was something of a status symbol.

Not so in the modern age. Today, share ownership is more popular than ever, and anyone who cares to do a little homework for themselves can find several ways of making potentially profitable investments - whether they want to invest a fortune or just a few hundred pounds or dollars.

This rise in the popularity of company shares has changed the face of private investment forever. Now many people are just as interested in finding out how their shares have fluctuated as they are in finding out what the latest weather forecast predicts. Indeed, millions of small investors are exploring the possibilities of the stock market as eagerly as NASA scientists explore the surface of Mars.

In short, share ownership has never been more popular.

Shares are bought and sold on the **stock-market**. This is much like any other market, but here the products on offer are stocks and commodities. Buying and selling is done through **brokers** who act as middle-men between prospective investors and the companies which have made their shares available to the public.

Why Do People Buy Shares?

There are many different types of shares available, and just as many reasons for buying them. Some people want to prepare financially for a future goal or event, such as retirement or the purchase of a home.

Others just want to make their savings work as hard as possible. Still others treat the stock market like a casino, buying and selling high-risk shares relatively rapidly in the hope of making big profits as quickly as possible.

In a nutshell, the benefits of shares can be summarised as follows:

✔ They can help an investor to make far more profit than he would if he left his money in a simple savings or bank deposit account.

✔ They can give the investor a great level of control over his personal finances.

✔ They can, over the long term, generate profits which vastly outperform normal interest rates.

Unfortunately, shares also have a major downside. Namely:

✘ Their values can go down as well as up, causing the investor to lose some or even all of their original investment.

The Key to Successful Investing

The key to successful investing in any financial product is to have a good level of knowledge. The more you know and understand about company shares and how to select them, the more chance you will have of showing a good profit over the long term. The main areas of knowledge you will need to develop are:

Product knowledge

There are many different types of shares and not all of them may be suitable for the achievement of any particular investment goal. Knowing which type of share is most suited to your investment needs is essential.

Arithmetical knowledge

Having some knowledge of simple arithmetical calculations will enable you to evaluate a company share before you actually decide whether or not to buy it. This will not only help you to save wasting time, but it will also help you confirm if the share in question is really worth buying in the first place.

Strategic knowledge

There are a number of different investment strategies which can help you to reduce the amount of risk you expose yourself to when dealing with company shares. Understanding these strategies and using them wisely could mean the difference between suffering a devastating loss or making a good profit.

Chapter One

Shares

A Working Definition

KEY FEATURE:
A share is exactly what the name suggests
- a share in the financial future of a company.

THE BASIC PRINCIPLE works like this: If a company is started by ten people who each invest $100, then the company is worth $1,000 and each **share-holder** owns one tenth of the whole. Should the company do well and make money, then each shareholder will receive a portion of the profits equal to their share-holding - in this case ten per cent each. This payout is called a **dividend**. Alternatively, the company directors may keep the profits in the company, in which case the value of the shares themselves will rise.

Let's say that the profits of this imaginary company are $500 for the year. Each investor will receive $50 by way of a dividend. Or, if the profits are retained, the company will be worth $1,500 and each share will have increased in value from $100 to $150.

If the company doesn't do well and actually loses $700 then the company is now worth just $300 and the value of each share will

---

have fallen from \$100 to just \$30. In addition, no dividend will be payable because no profits have been made.

Of course, this is just a theoretical example of how company shares work. In reality, there may be millions of share-holders for any one company and some of them will hold more shares than others. Nevertheless, the basic principle remains the same: shareholders receive a share of the company's profits or losses in direct proportion to the number of shares they own.

Why are company shares issued?

Shares are issued by companies for two major reasons. The first is to fund some kind of expansion, such as the building of a new production plant, opening a new research laboratory or broadening their product range. Issuing shares in the company helps to raise the necessary capital to achieve these aims, and will hopefully result in the company reaching a greater level of profitability.

The second major reason for issuing shares is to avoid taking out loans. Loans, whether taken from a bank or from the public via fixed interest securities, require a certain amount of interest to be paid regardless of how well or poorly the company performs in the coming years. If the company does well, that's fine, but if it doesn't do as well as it hopes, the interest on loans is still payable. Shareholders, however, would receive dividends which directly reflect the amount of profit the company makes. This means that if the company doesn't do so well, the dividends paid to shareholders would naturally be lower than any interest payable on a comparable loan.

From the investor's point of view, buying shares gives them a very real stake in the financial future of the company they invest in. If the company grows then their shares will increase in value and so will the dividends they receive each year. Of course, if the company fails then the value of their shares will fall - but that is the kind of risk a share investor is prepared to take in the hope of making potential profits.

Share Types

There are many kinds of shares available. The most common ones are:

- Ordinary Shares
- Preference Shares
- Cumulative Preference Shares
- Redeemable Preference Shares
- Convertible Preference Shares
- Zero Dividend Preference Shares (Zeros)
- Deferred Shares
- Bearer Shares
- Penny Shares

Each of these share types have their own key features and appeal to different types of investors, so now we will discuss each of them individually...

Ordinary Shares

Also referred to as equities, ordinary shares are the most common type of shares in the modern market. They give the share-holder the right to vote at share-holder meetings on the future of the company, normally on a vote-per-share basis. This means that for every share he holds, he has one vote. Ten shares equal ten votes, and so on.

All ordinary share-holders receive the same dividends in direct proportion to the size of their holdings. A person who owns 1,000 ordinary shares will therefore receive twice as much as someone who owns 500 shares, but only half as much as a person who owns 2,000 shares.

If a company is forced into liquidation, owners of ordinary shares are placed at the bottom of the list as far as payments to creditors are concerned. So it is quite possible that the ordinary share-holder may not get back any of his initial investment. This is a worst case scenario, but it is important to realise that it can happen all the same.

Ordinary shares issued by the very biggest companies are often referred to as blue chip shares. These are thought of as being as safe as ordinary shares can get, simply because blue chip companies have a track record of outstanding success and are not likely to disappear overnight.

Preference Shares

As their name suggests, preference shares give the share-holders preference over ordinary share-holders in the list of payments to creditors. This means that if a company goes into liquidation, a holder of preference shares will be paid before ordinary share-holders and so there is more chance of him recouping at least some of his initial investment.

Often, the dividend payable on preference shares is fixed and is not likely to fluctuate from year to year. There are some exceptions to this, however, and so you should always check the specific details of any preference share before buying.

Cumulative Preference Shares

These are the same as preference shares, with one major difference. If dividends have been unpaid at any point, the shareholder may be able to claim these dividends at a later date. Dividends are therefore said to be cumulative.

Redeemable Preference Shares

These have fixed repayment dates, allowing the investor to plan his financial affairs with some precision as far as time is concerned. Redeemable preference shares are more like loans than true shares, but currently the financial markets make no formal distinction.

Convertible Preference Shares

Convertible Preference Shares are interesting because they can be converted to ordinary shares on specific dates at predetermined rates. This means that if the company which issued convertible preference shares does particularly well, the shareholder has the opportunity (but not the obligation) to convert to ordinary shares and enjoy a capital gain.

Zero Dividend Preference Shares (Zeros)

'Zeros' are preference share with a fixed life. They form part of split capital investment trusts, provide no income, but as preference shares, have a prior entitlement to the assets of the trust when it is wound up. The redemption value and maturity date are known in advance, so Zeros are a useful way of ensuring a certain amount of capital at a certain time. Appropriate Zeros can be selected with the required maturity dates but are tradable on the stock market at any time.

Deferred Shares

These are shares which do not normally qualify for dividends until a predetermined date or profit level has been achieved by the company which issues them. They do, however, normally give the shareholder some of the benefits associated with other types of shares, such as the right to vote at shareholder meetings and some comeback in the event of the company in question going into liquidation.

Bearer Shares

As their name suggests, bearer shares belong to the person who holds (or "bears") the share certificate. Dividend payments are not sent out automatically but must be claimed by the bearer - normally by mailing a claim coupon. Bearer shares are more commonly used in other European countries than they are in the United Kingdom, but investors who want to keep their activities particularly discreet use them quite regularly since no register of shareholders is kept.

Penny Shares

There is no clear-cut definition of "a Penny Share". A decade ago investors may have said that a penny share was any share costing less than 30p or 50c. Today some say that a penny share is any share costing less than 90p or $1.50. These figures will undoubtedly be revised again in future years as shares in the broader market become more expensive. Penny shares are a subject in their own right and will be covered in much greater depth in Chapter Six.

Essential Terminology

Before closing this chapter and beginning a discussion on how the share market actually works, it is necessary to define some essential share-related terminology so that you fully understand what is being said later on in this book. Here then, is a crash-course in investment jargon...

Rights Issues

If a company has already issued shares but wishes to raise more capital, it may offer existing shareholders the opportunity to buy more. This is known as a rights issue.

Scrip Issues

If a company has already issued shares but wishes to increase the number of shares in circulation, it may give additional shares to existing shareholders on an "x for y" basis. This would be a scrip issue. For example, if a shareholder has ten £10 shares in a particular company, he may be given a scrip issue on a "five for one" basis. This might result in ten £10 shares being taken and replaced with fifty £2 shares. Note that because no additional capital has been injected into the company, the value of the new shares is proportionately decreased so that the shareholder neither gains or loses financially from the scrip issue.

New issues

When a company is floated on the stock exchange and offers shares for the very first time, these are said to be new issues.

Fixed Interest Stocks

Fixed interest stocks are normally referred to as either Bonds or
Gilts. A bond is a promise from a company to pay a lender of
money a fixed sum of interest on a regular basis for a stated
period. In other words, the person who invests in a bond is not
buying any equity in the company but is simply making a loan to
the company in return for a fixed sum of interest and a promise of
eventual repayment. A gilt is similar, but in this case the investor
lends money to the government to help the building of new
schools, roads and other projects which should improve the
productivity of the country.

Investing in fixed interest stocks is a specialist subject in its own
right. If you are interested in studying this subject further, please
refer to another book in this series entitled *Understand Bonds &
Gilts in a Day*.

Cum-Dividend

A stock or share which is described as being cum-dividend is one
which is being offered with the dividend included. For example,
if an investor buys a cum-dividend share one week before the
dividend payment date, he will receive all monies which have
accumulated since the last dividend payment date, even though
this may have been six months ago.

Ex-Dividend

A stock or share which is described as being ex-dividend is one
which is being offered with the dividend excepted. For example,
if our investor buys an ex-dividend share four months before the
next dividend payment date, he will not be entitled to receive a
dividend on that occasion.

Summary

✔ A share is exactly what the name suggests - a share in the financial future of a company.

✔ There are many kinds of shares available. The most common are: Ordinary Shares, Preference Shares, Cumulative Preference Shares, Redeemable Preference Shares, Convertible Preference Shares, Deferred Shares, Bearer Shares and Penny Shares.

✔ Ordinary shares issued by the very biggest companies are often referred to as **blue chip** shares.

✔ A stock or share which is being offered with the dividend included is commonly referred to as being cum-dividend.

✔ A stock or share which is being offered with the dividend excepted is commonly referred to as being **ex-dividend**.

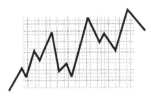

Chapter Two

Why Share Prices Fluctuate

KEY FEATURE:
We have all heard that, "shares can go down as well as up"
but few people talk about exactly why share prices fluctuate.
The purpose of this chapter is to throw a little light on the
subject by taking a brief look at how the stock market works.

SHARES ARE bought and sold on the stock market. This is - in theory - much like any other market; a place where buyers meet with sellers and deal-making is the order of the day. In a perfect world the only thing that should affect the price of shares is the performance of the companies which issue them. In reality the stock market is a little more complicated because demand for shares fluctuates from day to day due to a number of factors. These are:

● The general economic climate.

● The laws of supply and demand.

● The general mood of investors.

Each of these factors affects the stock market - and thus share prices - in different ways. To make these variable influences as easy as possible to understand, let us take a look at each one in turn...

The General Economic Climate

This is, to put it simply, the state of the country we live in from a financial point of view. The general economic climate is affected by wars, rumours of wars, unemployment figures, interest rates, current or pending political elections, the size of the national debt and a whole host of other imponderables. Unfortunately, few people ever really seem to agree as to what is, or is not, good for the economy.

For example, if the rate of unemployment increases dramatically, one group of doom-and-gloomers will predict the arrival of a new depression or recession. On the other hand, if the rate of unemployment decreases dramatically, another group of doom-and-gloomers will state that the economy is progressing too quickly and must be slowed down! So having said that, is unemployment good or bad for the economy?

This state of affairs is something which invariably baffles the new investor. What you should remember is; what the majority of investors *believe* about the economical climate often affects share prices more than the economy itself. For example, if the majority of investors are optimistic then more shares will be bought and prices will tend to rise.

By the same token, if the majority of investors are pessimistic then more shares will be sold and prices will tend to fall. This optimism and pessimism doesn't have to be based on any real economic data.

The Laws of Supply and Demand

The laws of supply and demand are the same in the stock market as they are in any other type of market. If there is a high demand for a certain product and supply is limited then prices will tend to rise, but if there is little demand for a product then prices will tend to fall.

Demand for certain types of shares tends to rise or fall according to how the underlying company performs. The shares of an established company which has good prospects for further growth or profitability will naturally be in higher demand than those of a company which is relatively new and has few prospects.

As with the general economic climate, what investors believe about the prospects of a company can affect share prices as much as any amount of hard data. Rumours that XYZ Cigarettes are to be successfully sued by a disgruntled smoker can send share prices plummeting because investors know that if the rumour is true, the cost of damages will affect the overall profitability of the company and open the floodgates for similar claims.

Similarly, rumours that ABC Avionics are about to be awarded with a mammoth contract from NASA can send share prices through the roof, simply because investors know that if the rumour is true profitability is sure to take an upward turn.

The General Mood of Investors

We have already referred to the general mood of investors twice in the last few minutes, and it must be said that this is what generates the majority of share price fluctuations. Let's face it, if share prices were determined solely by hard economic or corporate data then they would be far more stable than they are in actuality. The fact that share prices often fluctuate wildly despite hard data is proof that emotion is king as far as the stock market is concerned.

Emotions are impossible to quantify and even more difficult to predict, but a good idea of what the majority of investors think can be gained by paying close attention to the financial headlines in newspapers or on television news bulletins. These are the headlines which will be seen, read or heard by millions of investors - both private and professional - and undoubtedly have at least some effect on the direction the stock market takes.

To explain this situation, let us use the analogy of sheep and a shepherd. It is a rather crude analogy, but it sheds a great deal of light on the subject of share price fluctuations.

If you consider the masses of private investors to be sheep and the financial media to be a shepherd then it becomes clear that whichever direction the shepherd chooses to travel in, the sheep will surely follow. Of course, there is always the odd black sheep who goes against the trend, but in the main mass psychology will out and so financial headlines tend to become self-fulfilling prophecies.

For example, if a major financial journalist states that share prices are too high and will undoubtedly take a dramatic tumble in the near future, millions of sheep-like investors will take those words as gospel and act on them instinctively. They will sweat all night, call their brokers at first light and sell their holdings as quickly as possible. Supply drops off quite suddenly and naturally share prices do take the tumble that was predicted.

At this point everyone is sure that the financial journalist is a genius - if not a prophet - and so when he announces that the tumble is over and share prices are about to rocket, everyone piles back into the stock market. Demand soars, supply is limited and so share prices rise. The prophet scores two out or two for accuracy.

Because mass psychology has such a large effect on the stock market as a whole, patterns of rises, declines and crashes tend to repeat themselves quite dramatically over the long term. Certain patterns have been named and can be recognised quite readily when one knows what to look for. Here are the "big three" patterns which all investors should be aware of.

The Bull Market

A bull market is one in which share prices are on an upward trend. Share prices may dip for a day or week or two, but the underlying trend is upwards - often into new, uncharted territory. The illustration overleaf shows the share price of one imaginary company during a bull market. Note how the price goes down as well as up, but the overall trend is positive.

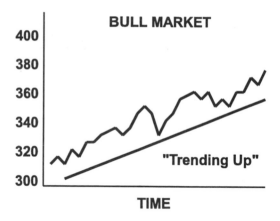

The average bull market lasts for around four years and general investing sentiment is usually quite positive.

Although some of the more pessimistic "gurus" of the investing world will warn of the impending down-trend which is "inevitable" even in the early months of a bull market, the majority of investors take confidence in the upward trend and continue buying shares even when hard data suggests that they are too expensive.

Towards the end of a bull market, the overall Price Earnings Ratio (see Chapter 9) tends to be very high and news of rising interest rates will have begun to hit the headlines. At this stage even good news has little further positive effect on share prices.

The Bear Market

A bear market is one in which share prices are on a downward trend. Share prices may rise for a day or week or two, but the underlying trend is undisputedly downwards. The illustration

above shows the share price of one imaginary company during a bear market. Note how the price goes up as well as down, but the overall trend is negative.

The average bear market lasts for around one year and general investing sentiment is usually quite negative. There is almost always talk from some quarters of the "inevitable" rise which lies just around the corner, but most investors avoid getting involved in the stock market through fear of suffering losses - even when hard data suggests that share prices are too low.

Towards the end of a bear market, the overall Price Earnings Ratio (again, see Chapter 9) tends to be very low and interest rates may begin to fall. At this stage even bad news has little further negative effect on share prices.

The Crash

A crash is commonly defined as a sharp fall in general share prices which reduces the overall value of the stock market by ten per cent or more. This is more of an event than a trend, but it is suitable for discussion here because a crash tends to follow a definite pattern.

To begin with, a crash normally happens when the vast majority of the investment world least expects it. Share prices will normally have been on an upward trend for quite some time on both sides of the Atlantic, often breaking into new, uncharted territory. During this time there will naturally have been some talk of how the market is due a "correction" of some kind, but in the main investor confidence will have been high. "This time things are different," many will say in response to the doom-and-gloomers.

And then, quite suddenly, the market suffers a massive drop. This could be due to bad economic news or some other event, but whatever sparks the initial fall in share prices, panic sets in and everyone heads for the exit. The phone lines to brokers become jammed as everyone desperately attempts to sell stock which no-one wants to buy, and the fall spirals rapidly.

However disastrous a stock market crash might appear, historical data indicates that recovery comes relatively quickly. *It took only two years to recover from the infamous stock market crash of 1987*, and if you look at this event from a wider perspective of ten or even five years it is apparent that the crash was merely a large and necessary correction to stabilise what had been quite a dramatic upward trend.

As long as an investor is taking the long term view, a crash is really not the end of the world. In fact after a crash has taken place there are almost always a variety of excellent opportunities to buy shares at ridiculously low prices, giving the potential for even greater profits in future years.

To buy, or not to buy?

That really is the question. With all of this talk of share price fluctuations, mass psychology, bull trends, bear trends and stock market crashes you might be forgiven for thinking that the answer is not to buy any shares to begin with. This is an attitude which many investors take, but in the long-term it is largely a self-defeating one. Consider the following:

● If you are actively investing in the stock market with a long term perspective then, although you may have to ride out a strong bear trend or perhaps even a crash, given time the probability is that your investments will recover and go on to make further profits.

● If you are deliberately avoiding stock market investment then, although you automatically avoid bear trends and any crash which may take place, you will also miss out on strong bull trends which have tremendous power to multiply your money.

If this is not enough to dispel any fear of downward cycles which the stock market may suffer, then perhaps you should consider this: there are a handful of advanced investment techniques which allow the investor to make good potential profits during good times and bad. In fact there is even a method of insuring your investments against the effect of crashes and strong bear trends. You will find these methods and techniques discussed in Chapter 10, but for now just remember that in order to win, you have to be in.

Summary

✔ Share prices fluctuate due to a number of factors, namely: the current economic climate, the laws of supply and demand and the general mood of investors.

✔ Mass psychology often affects the fluctuation of share prices as much - if not more so - than any other factor.

✔ Because mass psychology has such a large effect on the stock market as a whole, patterns of rises, declines and crashes tend to repeat themselves quite dramatically over the long term.

✔ A bull market is one in which share prices are on an upward trend. Share prices may dip from time to time, but the underlying trend is upwards. The average bull market lasts for around four years.

✔ A bear market is one in which share prices are on a downward trend. Share prices may rise from time to time, but the underlying trend is downwards. The average bear market lasts for around one year.

✔ A crash is commonly defined as a sharp fall in general share prices which reduces the overall value of the stock market by ten per cent or more. Historical data indicates that recovery from a crash usually comes relatively quickly.

Chapter Three

Buying and Selling Shares

KEY FEATURE:

Buying and selling shares is not as complicated as many people think. This chapter is designed to make the whole process much easier to understand.

PEOPLE BUY and sell shares for a wide variety of reasons. Some want to try and make their capital grow steadily over the long term but want a better return than they would get by putting their money into savings or deposit accounts. Others like the idea of investing in particular companies or sectors of companies due to a personal or professional interest in the same. Still others buy and sell shares simply because they like to speculate about - and hopefully profit from - market movements.

For whatever reason you wish to benefit from shares, you first have to buy them! Many high street banks offer a broker service whereby they will obtain or sell shares on behalf of their customers. For the occasional share investor this arrangement offers a lot in the way of convenience. All that is usually required is for the investor to complete a simple form which instructs the bank to buy or sell a specific number of shares in a certain company and then ensure that adequate funds are made available. This done, he can go home and get on with his life, secure in the knowledge that his bank will follow his instructions and buy or sell his shares accordingly.

Unfortunately, there are a number of down-sides to using a bank to buy or sell shares on a regular basis. These are as follows:

- The amount of commission and fees charged by banks for brokering services is often more than the amount charged by dedicated brokers. This is because share brokering is only one extra service as far as the bank is concerned, but a prime service as far as the broker is concerned.

- Buying and selling shares through a bank may be subject to a delay of anywhere between a few minutes and a few days. This means that the actual price of the share in question could go up or down before they are purchased or sold on behalf of the investor. Of course, this may work in the investor's favour (such as when a share price rises before a sell instruction is carried out) but it can equally work against him (such as when a share price rises before a buy instruction is carried out.) Dedicated brokers, on the other hand, tend to work on a more immediate basis with instant share-dealing being quite a common facility.

- Banks offer a variety of services, but they are best at banking. This is what they know best simply because this is what they do the most. The main occupation of a dedicated broker, on the other hand, is dealing with shares. This means that a dedicated broker is almost always more knowledgeable about the subject and is therefore in a better position to pass this knowledge on to the investor.

If you intend to deal in shares on anything other than an occasional basis, you would do well to consider doing your business via a dedicated broker rather than through a bank. A broker can make share dealing faster, less expensive and (depending on the type of broker you choose) a whole lot easier.

There are two types of brokers available to private investors. These are traditional and execution-only stockbrokers.

A **traditional stockbroker** will give his client advice, recommendations and market pointers in addition to buying or selling on the client's behalf. This advice can be extremely valuable for investors who are new to the world of shares, and will often help them avoid some of the mistakes which beginners often make. Because traditional stockbrokers do more than just buy and sell, the commissions they charge tend to be slightly higher than those charged by execution-only brokers - an additional expense which is often a price worth paying.

An **execution-only stockbroker** does not give his client any advice, recommendations or market pointers. He simply acts as the middleman between the investor and the market, buying and selling on his clients behalf. Execution only brokers usually offer the lowest commissions of all, but investors must be prepared to make their own decisions and live by the results.

If you are fully conversant with financial jargon, and understand the field you want to invest in thoroughly, then an execution-only broker may well meet your needs. Otherwise it would be better to err on the side of caution and deal through a traditional broker who will help you take your first steps into the market.

Selecting either a traditional or execution-only broker is largely a matter of making a short-list, discussing your requirements (and theirs) with each and then opting for the one which will be most suitable to your needs. Many brokers advertise in the financial press and also in more general directories such as The Yellow Pages. If you can, you should obtain references from any other private investors you know, since personal experience of a broker will often tell you more than any number of glossy brochures or pamphlets.

Once you have a short-list of brokers to contact, you then need to have a brief discussion with each so that you can determine if they are able (and willing) to offer you the kind of service you require. The main questions you need to ask any broker you are considering are:

What type of new clients are they accepting, if any?
Some brokers will only accept new clients who intend to put substantial amounts of business their way. Others are more than happy to accept small private investors. Discovering at the outset whether the broker you are talking to would be willing to take on your business might save you a great deal in the way of wasted time.

What are your commission rates?
Don't beat around the bush when it comes to talking about money - after all, this is what brokers talk about all day long. Most brokers charge commission according to a sliding scale. This

obviously means that the larger your investments are, the more commission you will pay. Almost all brokers establish a minimum commission fee which is payable on all transactions below a certain limit. Ask for both minimum commission details and sliding scale rates and this will help you to compare the broker with the others you contact.

Are there any other charges?
Often you won't need to ask this question because the broker will tell you about any additional fees when discussing commissions. If he doesn't, find out if he charges any management fees over and above the commission rates - most do. Some brokers who manage their clients' portfolios set fees which are related to the performance of the portfolio they control. This motivates them to make the best returns they can, so if you are aiming to have a broker take care of your portfolio and make your decisions for you, a fee which is directly related to performance might be a good thing.

What is your track record?
Some brokers are better than others when it comes to making money grow. Ask about past performance and you will get some idea of how useful his advice is. Obviously, if you are looking for an execution-only broker then you should not ask this question because no advice will be given and so past performance does not exist.

Once you have telephoned a few brokers and possibly leafed through any brochures they send you, a decision can be made on the basis of the information you have accumulated. Ask around your friends and acquaintances and see if you know anyone who has any personal recommendations. You can take these recommendations into account before making a final decision. Finally, if you are still unsure about which broker to use, consider consulting a professional financial advisor.

Registering with a Broker

Once you have found a suitable broker which you would like to deal with, you must then register as one of his clients. Normally this will involve little more than completing a few application forms and sending the broker a cheque which he can then invest according to your instructions. Sometimes however - especially if you want your broker to make your investment decisions for you - an informal meeting may be suggested so that you can discuss your objectives and investment preferences more fully in person.

Buying and Selling

When you have arranged to use the services of a broker, you are then free to start buying and selling shares and put your knowledge into practice. The majority of reliable brokers accept buy and sell instructions over the telephone, and this is the most convenient way of share dealing for all parties.

From the investor's point of view, buying and selling shares over the telephone has several distinct advantages over visiting a broker in person or dealing by one of the less common methods, such as by post:

● Telephone dealing is one of the most cost and time efficient methods of dealing in shares. No travel is involved (except perhaps to the nearest telephone kiosk!) and no appointments are necessary.

● Telephone dealing allows the investor to take advantage of stock market fluctuations as quickly as possible. This means that if the stock market begins to rise or fall dramatically, the investor can buy or sell shares in order to try and turn the trend into profit.

● Because a telephone call is so easy to make, an investor can usually contact his broker just to seek guidance (this service is not available from execution-only brokers) or information on his shares or prospective shares with no obligation to actually buy or sell.

● Telephone dealing allows investors to trade on a short-term basis if that is what they wish to do. For example, an investor could buy shares in the morning, watch them rise and then sell them a few hours later, taking a welcome profit in the process.

This is a more speculative approach to shares than many investors would like to take, but a growing number of people find this form of share dealing particularly fascinating - especially in volatile markets where profits (and it must be said, losses) can be made in a matter of hours.

Buying and selling shares over the telephone is a fairly simple matter and often takes just a few minutes. Once a decision has been reached about which shares an investor wants to buy or sell (according to his own knowledge or the advice of his broker) he is normally asked to give the broker the following information:

● His account number with the broker.

● The name (and type, if applicable) of the shares he wishes to deal in on this occasion.

● His instructions as to whether he wishes to buy shares or sell existing ones.

● The quantity of shares he wishes to buy or sell.

The broker may then tell the investor the 'price' at which the shares are trading and selling for, and ask if these are agreeable. This 'price' will be quoted as two figures, such as 100-104. The lower figure is the **bid quote** - an indication of how much will be paid to the investor for each share sold (100p). The higher figure is the **offer quote** - an indication of how much it will cost the investor to buy each share (104p). The difference between the two quoted figures is known as **the spread**.

It is important to realise that occasionally just one figure is given in newspapers and some other sources. This is known as the **mid-price** and is, as the term suggests, the mid point of the bid offer spread. The mid-price for the above quoted share would therefore be 102.

You should note that the share prices quoted are hardly ever guaranteed and can fluctuate even before the broker has a chance to hang up the telephone. The **striking price** (the price at which a shares deal is actually struck) may therefore differ from the prices quoted on the telephone. An investor can get around this fact by instructing his broker not to buy or sell above or below a particular price. This allows the investor to know for definite the maximum amount of money the deal will cost if executed.

Once all of these points have been confirmed (the telephone conversations to brokers are usually recorded in case a dispute arises) then that is all there is to it. The deal has been made. Within a few days the investor will receive a contract note, which is a written confirmation of his transaction and, presuming that this is correct, it may be filed to serve as a permanent record. Finally, if shares have been bought, a share certificate will be sent to the investor direct from the company registrars as legal proof of his purchase.

Dealing Online

Whilst telephone dealing is still the preferred method for the majority of investors, and it is likely to remain so in the future, a new way of buying and selling shares has emerged over the last couple of years. Dealing online (via the Internet) allows you to cut costs dramatically and speeds up transaction times. However, there are drawbacks. You'll find a fuller discussion in Chapter 14.

Buying and selling shares is not as complicated as many people tend to think. Once you have access to the services of a broker and understand the various prices and terms which are quoted, actually dealing is a simple matter of issuing appropriate instructions.

Summary

✔ If you intend to deal in shares on anything other than an occasional basis, you would do well to consider doing your business via a **dedicated broker**.

✔ There are **two types** of brokers available to private investors. These are traditional stockbrokers and execution-only stockbrokers.

✔ A **traditional stockbroker** will give his client advice, recommendations and market pointers in addition to buying or selling on the client's behalf.

✔ An **execution-only stockbroker** does not give his client any advice, recommendations or market pointers. He simply acts as the **middleman** between the investor and the market, buying and selling on his clients behalf.

✔ Selecting either a traditional or execution-only broker is largely a matter of making a short-list, discussing your requirements with each and then opting for the one which will be most suitable to your needs.

✔ Brokers often quote **two figures** to prospective investors. The lower figure is the **bid** quote - an indication of how much will be paid to the investor for each share sold. The higher figure is the **offer** quote - an indication of how much it will cost the investor to buy each share. The difference between the two quoted figures is known as the **spread**.

✔ The price at which the actual shares are bought or sold is known as the **striking price**.

Chapter Four

Unit and Investment Trusts - Mutual Funds

KEY FEATURE:
Unit Trusts and Mutual Funds are investment vehicles which are designed to help the investor spread his risk and pool his financial resources with other investors.

SPREADING YOURSELF over a wide area is often the best way to avoid calamity. Consider a pond which is frozen over. If you need to reach something in the middle of the pond you can either walk across the ice and risk breaking through the surface, or you can lie down and slither towards the object. This second method has the effect of spreading your body weight fairly evenly over a larger area of ice, thus reducing the risk of the ice breaking underneath you.

This analogy works quite well in the world of stock market investment in that there are two main methods of trying to secure profits. You can either pour your money into just a few shares and hope that they are strong enough to help you make the profits you want, or you can spread your money over a broad variety of shares in order to spread risk and - hopefully - reduce the risk of losses.

Unfortunately, few private investors have the financial wherewithal to invest in a wide range of companies and still stand a chance of achieving a good level of capital growth. Part of the reason being the costs involved with dealing. If you are starting with $10,000, then the most shares you can practicably invest in is around 10. Otherwise the cost of buying each set of shares will eat up a larger percentage of your original cash.

For this reason many people pool their financial resources by putting their money in a pooled investment of some kind. This chapter discusses how this pooling of resources works, the types of pooled investments available and the pros and cons of each.

Unit Trusts

A Unit Trust is an investment vehicle in which money from a group of investors is pooled and used to create a diverse portfolio on their behalf. Each investor is allocated a number of units according to the size of his original investment and will receive the relevant proportion of profits after all costs and charges have been taken into consideration. To illustrate how this works in practice, consider the following example...

A trust invests £5 Million in a wide variety of stocks and securities. It splits this portfolio into 1,000 separate units. Each unit therefore costs £5,000.

The portfolio does well and the £5 Million grows to some £8 Million. Each unit is now worth £8,000 (£8m divided by 1,000 units = £8,000) and so any investor who bought a unit at the original price of £5,000 will have made £3,000 profit before charges. What is more, the individual investors have left all of the investment decisions and portfolio management to the unit trust company.

Individual investors can leave unit trusts at any time by selling their units, but this type of investment vehicle should primarily be seen as medium to long term investment. Similarly, investors can increase their holdings by purchasing further units whenever they want. The cost of units, however, will obviously rise and fall according to the performance of the trust itself.

The main advantages of investing in Unit Trusts are:

✔ An individual investor can spread his money over a much wider range of securities in a unit trust than would be possible if he built his own portfolio of shares (see Chapter 5). This is because the unit trust is a pool of money, and something like £5 Million from 1,000 separate investors can be spread more thinly than a much smaller individual fund of £5,000.

✔ Some unit trusts encourage investors by allowing people to invest small sums on a regular (usually monthly) basis as well as, or instead of, in lump sums. Thus it is possible to take advantage of a unit trust with an investment which can often be as small as £25 per month.

✔ Unit Trusts are handled by professional fund managers, so the individual investors do not have to make any specific portfolio management decisions.

Before deciding to get involved with any particular unit trust, you must bear in mind that different unit trusts will have different performance records. Some unit trusts have done extremely well in the past whilst others have not done so well. Of course, past performance cannot be taken as a guarantee of what might happen in the future. But large investment houses employ teams of people to manage the trust's assets and these teams build up certain investment know-how which will not disappear overnight. So it makes sense that you should look to join a winning team if you decide to join one at all.

Investment Trusts
- Mutual Funds

Investment trusts (becoming more commonly known as Mutual Funds) are companies which exist specifically for the purpose of investing in other companies. Like most other large companies, they issue shares and are quoted on the stock market in their own right.

The main difference between a unit trust and an mutual fund from the investor's point of view is that a mutual fund has a greater number of options as far as generating profits are concerned. As well as investing in the shares of other quoted companies, a mutual fund may also:

❑ Buy shares in unquoted companies

❑ Generate money by investing in derivative products (see Chapter 11)

❑ Invest in property

❑ Borrow money for investment purposes

In fact, a mutual fund can virtually generate money in whatever way it chooses, within certain limits. This is because, unlike a unit trust, it is a company in its own right and not merely a pool of money.

Another difference is the fact that unit trusts are **open-ended**, whilst mutual funds are **closed-ended**. This means that once all the shares in a mutual fund have been sold, no more will be made available. Unit trusts, on the other hand, can take in as much 'new' money as it wishes.

The fact that more shares in a mutual fund trust will not be issued creates price fluctuations as demand rises and falls - just like any other share. Unit trusts, however, fluctuate in price depending on the value of the shares owned by the trust. Mutual funds are commonly valued every month, whilst unit trust values are calculated daily.

Investing in a mutual fund is a simple matter of buying its shares. Some mutual funds go even further and set up a savings plan whereby investors can benefit from their abilities with either monthly or lump-sum investments.

Mutual funds which offer a monthly savings facility are very popular with people who are new to the idea of stock market investment, but - as always - professional financial advice is recommended before a decision to get involved is made.

Loaded or No Load?

Mutual Funds are often described as either **Loaded** Mutual Funds or **No Load** Mutual Funds. In both cases, the word "load" can be taken to mean sales charge. A loaded mutual fund has a sales charge which the investor must pay, whilst a no-load mutual fund does not have a sales charge.

Loaded mutual funds can be described as front-end loaded or back-end loaded. The difference is as follows:

Front-End Loaded

A front-end loaded mutual fund has a sales charge which is paid when the investor originally buys shares in the fund. For example, if there is a front-end load of 6% and you invest $1,000 in the fund, $60 will be taken in charges and only the remaining $940 will actually be invested on your behalf.

Back-End Loaded

A back-end loaded (or **deferred load**) mutual fund has a sales charge which is paid when you sell your shares in the fund. Commonly, this starts at around 6% and decreases in line with the age of your investment, usually falling to 0% after around seven years. Thus, if you invest $1,000 in a back-end loaded mutual fund and sell your shares in that fund just a few months later, you will usually have to pay 6% in sales charges. You will therefore receive back just $940. If you leave your money in the fund longer, and the sales charge reduces to 0%, you will receive every cent of your investment and, of course, any growth which that investment has enjoyed over the period.

Summary

✔ **Spreading yourself** over a wide area is often the best way to avoid calamity, and that is the basic principle on which unit trusts and mutual funds are built.

✔ A **Unit Trust** is an investment vehicle in which money from a group of investors is **pooled and used to create a diverse portfolio** on their behalf.

✔ A Mutual Fund (or Investment Trust) is a company which exists specifically for the purpose of investing in other companies. **Mutual Funds issue their own shares** and are quoted on the stock market in their own right.

✔ If a Mutual Fund is described as **loaded** then the investor must pay a **sales charge**.

✔ If a mutual Fund is described as **no-load** then the investor does **not have to pay a sales charge**.

✔ No part of the sales charge is invested on behalf of the investor in the mutual fund, since it is really just a commission paid to the brokerage company handling the fund.

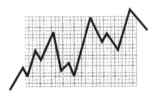

Chapter Five

Building a Share Portfolio

KEY FEATURE:

A portfolio is a varied collection of investments which through diversity give a certain element of stability. They are usually built with a specific objective in mind.

THE LAST chapter explained that the best way to reduce the risk of calamity is to spread your investments over a wide area. It also said that pooled investments can help an individual to take this approach and diversify his share-holdings.

Pooled investments, however, are not the only way of spreading risk. Given adequate investment capital you can build your own portfolio of shares which balances higher-risk holdings with those of lower risk. By doing this you hope to achieve steady long-term capital growth without having all of your eggs in one basket.

For example, Mr Wynne wants to invest in shares in order to help him prepare for retirement in ten years time. He has $50,000 to invest, so he could build a portfolio of shares which would offer him good returns and good security at the same time. He could split his $50,000 into perhaps twenty separate funds of $2,500 and

---

make twenty different investments - some in blue-chip shares for security and some in new issues for higher potential gains.

By spreading his total portfolio capital of $50,000 over twenty different investments, Mr Wynne would effectively be spreading his risks. If a handful of shares go down, others may increase in value and so offset the loss. If he had invested the whole $50,000 into just one company, however, the loss could be catastrophic. Of course this is a highly simplistic view of how a portfolio works, but it does serve to illustrate how portfolios can be used to help spread risks quite thinly.

A well diversified portfolio can help to give your investments a general balance between risk and reward, but diversification can also help to smooth any delays between the interest payments you receive on your individual holdings.

Of course, it would be foolish for any investor to put all of his money in shares. A share portfolio should be just one part of a larger financial plan. This larger financial plan should be organised so that a careful balance of low-, medium- and high-risk investments is maintained at all times. This approach (called *The Pyramid Principle*) is explained in more detail in my companion book *Understand Bonds and Gilts in a Day*, but the principles are well worth repeating here.

The Pyramid Principle states that the investments of any individual or organisation should be set up in such a way so that there is a balance of risk. There should be three sections to this investment pyramid - a wide foundation of very secure, low yield investments, a smaller mid-section of medium risk, medium reward investments and an even smaller peak of higher risk investments which give the potential for even higher gains. The pyramid would therefore look something like this:

The purpose of The Pyramid Principle is to try and ensure that no investor - either private or corporate - becomes "top heavy" by taking on a lot of high risk investments without first having a solid base and mid-section of low and medium risk investments. Let's look at these three sections of low, medium and high risk in turn and see how they apply to the share investor.

Low Risk Base

This is money which is as secure as can be. Deposit account savings and government bonds fall into this range. These vehicles generally offer only small potential rewards but give the investor a very good element of capital safety. Corporate fixed interest stocks would fall into this category because they are loans rather than purchases of equity, so the risk of losing money is fairly low.

No investor should contemplate taking on medium or high risks until he has first built a dependable low risk base of capital which - although probably not earning a great deal - can be relied on whatever the markets may be doing.

Medium Risk Mid-Section

Medium risk investments are those which offer more potential rewards but still leave most of the capital fairly secure. Unit Trusts are generally said to be in this range. So are blue chip shares issued by solid, reliable companies which are least likely to go into liquidation and are likely to show good profits over the long term.

The Medium risk section of the pyramid is designed to give the investor a higher level of return without taking very big risks. Again, until you have built this section of your pyramid you shouldn't get involved in the next level, which are high-risk investments.

High Risk Peak

High risk investments include derivatives (see Chapter 11), penny shares (see Chapter 6) and others which give the potential - though certainly not a promise - for extremely high rewards. This high-risk peak should only be built when the earlier sections of your pyramid have been established. Investing in high-risk investments before that point could ruin you financially if things go wrong.

Going back to our example of Mr Wynne; a good application of The Pyramid Principle might be for him to have fifty per cent of his money in lower-risk deposit accounts or government bonds, forty per cent in a medium risk share portfolio and just ten per cent in derivatives, penny shares and other high-risk investments. If this happened, the share portfolio would, when illustrated graphically, sit in the medium-risk mid-section of the pyramid structure, as follows:

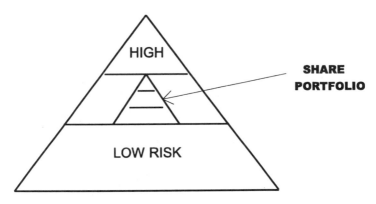

For a share portfolio to be effective, it should be designed with a specific aim in mind. This will help to clarify the investor's position at any given moment and adjust the portfolio as and when it becomes necessary. Here we will take a look at the specific financial goal of accumulating long-term savings, and consider how a share portfolio might help this be achieved...

Long Term Savings

We all have things that we would like to purchase in the future, and we have future events which need to be planned for if they are to be paid for. A share portfolio can help to finance these purchases and/or events if it is geared for capital growth over the long term. What's more, the portfolio can be built according to the desired risk level of the investor.

- For the investor who wants to take a relatively low level of risk, a suitable portfolio might mix a good proportion of fixed-interest stocks with a few hand-picked blue-chip shares to help boost potential gains.

- For the investor who wants to take a medium risk in order to achieve his goals, a suitable portfolio might focus on a variety of blue-chip shares which, although unlikely to generate vast profits, are equally unlikely to lose their value quite so quickly as higher-risk shares.

- For the investor who would like to take a higher level of risk, a suitable portfolio could focus on new issues which have the potential for greater profits and counterbalance these with more stable blue-chip shares.

Sleeves up and hands on

It is vitally important that all investors see their portfolios as highly flexible organisms which can and should be adapted to suit any changing economic situations and/or any change in the desired risk level. The investor should review the performance of his or her portfolio on an annual basis at the very least to ensure that it is on target to meet the pre-determined goals. If it is not then the portfolio should be thoroughly revised and under-performing shares should be sold in favour of those that hold more promise. Of course, the balance of risk and reward must continue to be maintained.

If you are not willing to roll up your sleeves and take a hands-on approach to maintaining your portfolio then you should leave this to someone else. You could either employ the services of a professional portfolio manager or, alternatively, invest your money in a unit trust or mutual fund.

When all is said and done, building and maintaining a well-balanced portfolio is one of the best ways for an investor to spread his risk without having to pool resources or call on the services of a professional.

Of course, managing a portfolio properly involves being able to value the shares within it, monitor stock market movements and then act appropriately. To help you decide if this is something you wish to do for yourself, there is a discussion of professional methods for share evaluation and analysis later in the book.

Summary

- ✔ A **portfolio** is a varied **collection of investments** which, through diversity, give a certain element of **stability**. Most portfolios are built with a specific objective in mind.

- ✔ A well **diversified** portfolio can help give your investments a general balance between risk and reward.

- ✔ Portfolios should be well balanced and follow the **pyramid structure**, mixing low, medium and higher risk investments.

✔ You should **review the performance** of your portfolio on an annual basis at the very least to ensure that it is on target to meet your goals.

✔ Managing a portfolio properly involves being able to value the shares within it, **monitor stock market movements** and then act appropriately.

Chapter Six

Penny Shares

KEY FEATURE:
A Penny Share is commonly said to be one which has a low price in relation to the broader market.

INVESTORS, WHO WANT to know why penny shares are seen by many people as being one of the most exciting types of shares, should look first at the example of Polly Peck in the early 1980s. Shares in this company were available for just 9p each at one time, but three years later they were valued at an incredible £35. This meant that a £900 investment in the original penny shares grew to some £350,000 - a mammoth profit - for those who got out before the company went belly up.

A more recent example is the emergence of 'dot com' stocks in the opening months of the year 2000. Penny shares were floated on little more than a wing and a prayer. Many zoomed upwards to fall disastrously by the end of the year. In 2001, investors who held on were nursing their wounds. Dramatic increases in value don't happen every day but a 12p or 20p share sometimes shows a rapid and phenomenal growth. In the USA shares costing a dollar or less have later rocketed to $10 or $20 in much less time than might be normally imagined.

The reverse happens too, particularly with technology stocks. Some trading at high levels in the boom period of the year 2000, became penny shares in 2001. As an example, in June 2001, QXL shares were trading in the UK stock market at around 10p. A year earlier they cost £7.44.

The most attractive thing about penny shares is the seemingly unlimited growth potential of a real winner. They are, however, high-risk investments suitable only if you are prepared to lose most or even all of your investment as happened to luckless Polly Peck investors.

To avoid this scenario, check with the Ombudsman or other relevant authority to see if any compensation is available. Otherwise, you are on your own. Do not hold a losing investment to the bitter end. To stand a decent chance of penny share success, cut losses quickly and let profits run. Penny shares are definitely NOT suitable for the faint-hearted.

What gives penny shares their potential?

It might seem odd that a share costing less than a daily newspaper could triple or quadruple its value in a short while, whilst a share costing many times more may only grow a little over the same period. But if you look at the matter closely the apparent paradox is quite easy to understand.

Consider a share in a blue-chip company. The company has been around for years and has grown from a small-time producer of widgets to the world's leading brand. It has expanded all it can, and there is little room for further growth. All it can really hope for is that widgets become more popular and that this popularity helps to increase the market demand for their products still further.

A penny share company is an entirely different proposition. The company is likely to be fairly new and relatively small. Its product may not yet have caught the public eye, and many people won't even have heard of the company itself. From this point the company can usually do one of two things:

● Fail and fall into even further obscurity, if not out of business altogether.

● Succeed and grow at a relatively dramatic rate.

Obviously, if the company fails then even the penny shares will fall in value. Occasionally a penny share can become virtually worthless in these situations simply because there are few people willing to buy them. But if the company succeeds and perhaps lands an important contract which increases the interest of more "mainstream" investors, then the share price can easily double, treble, quadruple and go on to create massive gains for its early penny share investors.

Therefore a penny share has more **potential** for profits simply because the company which issues it tends to have more potential for growth, expansion and greater success in the business world.

High risk, high reward?

Penny shares are high-risk, high reward investments and definitely not for the faint-hearted. But whilst this may technically be true, the risk and reward ratio should be examined in greater detail, since there are benefits to investing in penny shares which most people overlook.

To begin with, the potential losses on a penny share investment are always known at the outset. If you buy 1,000 shares at 50c then you could - if the bottom dropped out of the world - lose $500. Whilst this loss is a seemingly frightening one hundred per cent of your initial investment, it is often not nearly as much as you might lose on a blue-chip investment should things go wrong. For example, if you buy 1,000 shares at $11.50 and the share price falls by ten per cent, your original investment of $11,500 will now only be worth only $10,350 - a loss of $1,150. Thus a ten per cent fall on a blue chip share can sometimes damage your pocket more than a total loss on a penny share.

Looking at the situation from the other side of the fence, the potential gains from a penny share can be enormous. The glowing example of Polly Peck is a case in point. Just £90 invested in PP shares at 9p each would have grown to £3,500 just three years later. Compare this enormous return with what you might gain out of a blue-chip investment over the same period and the difference is clear.

Of course, no one would suggest that an investor should focus entirely on penny shares unless they really are prepared to ride the rough with the smooth. Adding a few penny shares to a more conservative portfolio would, however, give the potential for greater returns without breaking the bank should they fail to meet expectations.

Selecting penny shares

Succeeding with penny shares is simply a matter of picking the winners and avoiding the losers. Of course, this is easier said than done, but there are a couple of pointers which you might like to consider:

● Most penny share experts agree that assets are the most important consideration when looking for winners. The more assets a company has (in the form of property, machinery, etc.) the better. Occasionally you will find shares which are worth less than the actual assets of the company, so if the worst happened and the liquidators moved in, there would be more than enough money generated by the sale of these assets to cover your original outlay - and perhaps a bit more besides.

● Technical analysis (see Chapter 10) may help to provide clues about possible winners. But with penny shares in particular it is important to pay equal attention to more fundamental analysis, such as the amount of money the company has in the bank, etc.

If you are serious about wanting to tap into the potential of penny shares you would undoubtedly benefit greatly by studying some of the excellent books available on the subject. Some companies also issue tip-sheets and newsletters which are designed to highlight probable winners and losers.

Make no mistake, penny shares are more **volatile** than the average blue-chip shares which make headlines. This volatility has helped some investors to make gargantuan profits in the past. The same can happen in the future.

If you are prepared to take a higher level of risk in the hope of making a potentially higher gain, penny shares may be worth their weight in gold.

Summary

✔ A **Penny Share** is commonly said to be one which has a **low price in relation to the broader market**.

✔ Penny shares are **high-risk investments** which are only suitable if you are prepared to lose - in a worse case scenario - every penny of your investment. Of course, the same caution should be applied to all shares.

✔ The main advantage of penny shares is that **their value can multiply many times** over in a relatively short time.

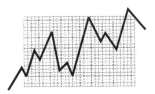

Chapter Seven

Reading the Financial Press

> **KEY FEATURE:**
> *The financial press is a valuable source of information which no serious or aspiring investor can afford to overlook. Knowing how to get the most out of the valuable resource can be a major key to your long-term success.*

THE DIFFERENCE between success and failure in any venture is often the quality of information at hand, and share investment is no exception to this general rule. The more you know about the share market, the shares available and the companies which issue them, the greater your chances of long term success.

The best source of share-related information in the UK can be found in financial publications such as the *Financial Times* and *Investors Chronicle*, but other daily newspapers also carry a substantial amount of share price information. In the USA, investors will more naturally turn to *The Wall Street Journal*. In addition to specific company and share information, specialist financial publications also feature many articles and news snippets about general economic items which can be of enormous use.

This chapter will take a brief look at the main items of interest to any share investor, and in doing so, illustrate how you can get the most out of the financial press...

Headlines

It has already been said that the majority of investors are like sheep who act on herd instincts, buying or selling according to what everyone else is doing. The headlines in the financial press are one of the factors which affect this mass psychology in the first place, so you must pay attention to what they are saying.

It is obvious that not all headlines will agree, but again, the majority tends to rule. If seven out of ten headlines state that the stock market is heading for a crash then roughly seven out of ten people will believe this to be so and act on that belief as though it was a foregone conclusion. They will therefore tend to sell their shares rather than buy any more. Conversely, if the majority of headlines predict a stock market boom then you might expect the majority of investors to be more interested in buying than in selling.

Studying the headlines of the financial press can help you gauge what the majority of investors will be thinking during any given period, and thus give you an insight into how the stock market will react.

Share Prices

The closing prices of specific shares are central statistics which no investor can afford to ignore. They allow you to keep track of which shares are rising and which shares are falling, and are vital if you intend to use **Technical Analysis** (see Chapter 10) to help you make your investment decisions.

Typically, shares are listed in groups, according to which sector of the market they are associated with. For example, television broadcasting companies and record companies tend to be listed under a heading such as "MEDIA" whilst computer manufacturing companies and retailers tend to be listed under "ELECTRICALS" or something similar. Knowing this can help you find the shares you are interested in quickly without having to wade through pages of listings.

The share details themselves normally comprise of at least five components, which are:

● The name of the company issuing the shares.

● The current share price.

● The change from the previous trading day.

● The share price high.

● The share price low.

This data might be set out as follows:

	Price	**Change**	**Hi**	**L**
Invisible Widgets	303	+7	303	270

This would mean that:

1. The ordinary shares issued by a company called Invisible Widgets stand at 303p each. This is the **mid-price**, so if you were to buy these shares they may actually cost a little more (say 305p), and if you were to sell them you may get back a little less (say 301p). Share prices given in any publication are for informational purposes only, and errors and omissions do occur, so you must always check the prices with your broker before buying or selling.

2. The next item of data tells you that the shares rose by 7p on the day. This means that the previous day's closing mid-price must have been 296p per share.

3. The third item tells you that the highest the shares have been is 303p per share. So Invisible Widgets' shares are currently trading at their highest level.

4. The final item tells you that the lowest the shares have been is 270p per share.

Sometimes other data is given, such as the open, day hi and day lo figures. These are simply the prices of the shares when the market opened and at the highest and lowest points on a particular day.

Investment Tips

Almost every newspaper prints investment "tips" of one kind or another. These are buy or sell suggestions for certain shares and attract a massive following despite the fact that they are not to be construed as financial advice in the real sense of the phrase. Indeed, so many people follow the investment tips of particular publications that they too can tend to become **self-fulfilling prophecies**.

For example, if a tip is published in a popular Sunday newspaper to buy shares in Ocepoc Media Plc, millions of people will read that tip and thousands will act on it. The number of people who actually buy the shares will depend largely on how much the tipster is respected by the investing public, but you can be fairly sure that the share price will rise, at least for a short time, simply because of all the new buyers which the tip has generated. Similarly, a sell tip can cause the price of the share in question to fall over the next day or two.

Knowing what has been tipped as a buy or sell in the financial pages can be worth its weight in gold to the speculative investor who aims to generates profits by predicting share price movements, but that will be discussed further in Chapter 11.

Director Dealings

It makes sense that the people who are intimately involved with a particular company are likely to know more about it than the average investor. For this reason, many publications print a list of the most notable "Director Dealings".

These are the shares bought or sold by directors of the company in question, and they reveal whether the people actually running the company are happy to increase their investment in it or are looking to reduce their holdings.

Director Dealings
Ocepoc Plc   £350,000

Here, £350,000 has been invested by the director(s) in our fictitious company Ocepoc Plc. To many investors this is a significant transaction and could suggest that the director knows something that they don't in order to warrant such a large investment. Some private investors will therefore take a closer look at this company with a view to jumping aboard the band wagon and getting a slice of the action themselves.

Note the phrase, "a closer look" in that last paragraph. To buy or sell shares based solely on director dealings would be foolish. But such dealings, whether they are positive or negative, can and should be followed up with further study of the company in question. If this study concludes that the shares are indeed worth buying or selling, then the investor can act on this informed opinion.

Results Due

Almost all financial publications print a list of companies which are due to publish their final (annual) or interim (usually six monthly) accounts. Sometimes they also include an estimate of how much they think the **Earnings Per Share (EPS)** are likely to be.

Knowing which companies are due to publish their results is, in itself, of little importance. But if this schedule is read in conjunction with the table of Director Dealings, the investor can often put two and two together and come up trumps.

For example, if you have noted that a director of Ocepoc Plc has purchased £350,000 worth of shares in the last week, and that this company is due to publish its annual results next week, you might conclude that good news is on the horizon.

This might explain why the director has made such a large investment, because if the results are good, he knows that the world and his wife will want to buy shares in his company, thus pushing the price up. By purchasing £350,000 of shares before the publication of the results, he can benefit from this increase in share price almost automatically.

Of course, if the director had sold £350,000 of shares, then you might conclude that the results may not be very good. In this case it is likely that the director has sold his shares because he thinks they will soon go down in value.

Again, you are dealing here with clues to, not promises of, what might happen in the future. It is always advisable to take financial advice before making any investment decision, particular if you are new to the stock market.

Make no mistake, learning how to read the financial press properly will allow you to take **full advantage** of what is, after all, a very economical resource. Begin paying attention to headlines, share prices, investment tips, director dealings and results due tables and you will find that, with a little practice, you can piece these items together like a jigsaw to provide a very comprehensive picture of the market as a whole.

Summary

✔ The **financial press** is a valuable source of information which no serious or aspiring investor.can afford to overlook.

✔ **Headlines** in the financial press are one of the factors which affect the mass **psychology of investors**, so you must pay attention to what they are saying.

✔ **Share prices** allow you to keep track of which shares are rising and which shares are falling, and are vital if you intend to use Technical Analysis to help you make your investment decisions.

✔ **Investment tips** are followed by thousands of people and, at the very least, can often be seen as **self-fulfilling prophecies**.

✔ **Director Dealings** are printed in most financial publications and these can give you some **insight** as to what may lie in store for a company - particularly if they are studied in conjunction with a Results Due table.

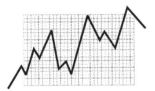

Chapter Eight

Reading Company Accounts

KEY FEATURE:
Company Accounts may look tedious, but they contain useful information which can give you the edge.

COMPANIES ARE legally bound to produce a set of accounts every year. These are sent out a few weeks before the Annual General Meeting (AGM). They include a notice of the meeting (venue, date, time) and the motions on which shareholders can vote, for example a rights issue or increase of directors' fees. Also included are reports from auditors, directors and chairman and key financial items:

- The **profit and loss account**,
- The **balance sheet**, and
- The **cash flow statement**.

If you are a shareholder, you will be sent the accounts a few weeks before the AGM. Copies are also available to non-shareholders upon application to the companies themselves or their registrars.

Interim results come out before the annual report, contain much of the same information, are widely quoted in the press, but not audited. They show a company's profitability, or otherwise, in the first six months of the year, the interim balance sheet, a cash flow statement and perhaps an interim dividend announcement.

What Do All Those Words Mean?

Many investors, perhaps put off by the figures and the jargon, do not read any of this material and so miss out on vital information. Although some annual accounts may be slightly secretive or misleading, most of them can help you make decisions on whether to buy, sell or hold on to a share.

Even if you are 'in for the long term', it is worthwhile looking at the annual accounts for the information they contain. Start with the easier bit: that is the chairman's, auditors' and directors' reports.

Spot the Truth

It is not always possible to spot the companies that are heading for a fall and taking their shareholders with them. Even very reputable accountancy firms who audit the accounts are not infallible. They can be misled by companies who have something to hide. Assuming everything on the surface looks OK, the auditors want the audit for the next year. So investors need to keep a healthy scepticism about the annual report even when a company seems solid enough. Occasionally a mention of the company in the newspapers hints at impending doom.

At first sight, these might seem the ideal bedtime reading for insomniacs but they often give clues which unravel those vital financial items: the profit and loss account, the balance sheet and the cash flow statement

The Chairman's Report

The chairman's message is usually on the front page. It might be as imaginative as a *Mills and Boon* romance but the Chairman also has to keep his head when all about him might be losing theirs; a gloomy message sends the share price tumbling no matter what the future holds. Here is a typical chairman's message beginning with the usual salutation:

Dear Shareholder
I am pleased to enclose the first annual report for XYZ Company. In addition, you will find the notice of Annual General Meeting (AGM) together with notes explaining the business of the AGM.

The chairman then goes on to say that *the company now has a policy of not paying any dividends.* (This will show up in the accounts). *As compensation, smaller investors, that is those holding 1000 or less shares will be able to sell them **without** incurring any fees for approximately three months after this message is sent out. Thereafter the charge will be £x.* The message usually ends with some optimistic words about enhancing shareholder value.

So far so good, but the fact that dividends are no longer being paid, means that investors who hold shares for income rather than growth might well be advised to invest somewhere else with better income prospects.

Auditors' Report

Auditors check that the company is a going concern. After outlining the respective responsibilities of directors and auditors, they report that they have conducted their work in accordance with bulletin 1999/6 of the Auditors Practices Board. If everything appears satisfactory, the financial statement is then said to comply *'with the applicable requirements of section 2552 of the Companies Act 1985 and the regulations made thereafter.'* This shows that even if the company is a tortoise rather than a hare, investors and others can assume that it is not trying to defraud or deceive anybody.

In our example of the XYZ Company, the auditors' report is fairly typical. It says that the financial statement of the Group *'was unqualified and did not contain any statement under sections 237(2) of the Companies Act 1985 such as inadequate records or returns, accounts not agreeing with records and returns, or failure to obtain necessary information and explanations'.*

If there are any inadequacies, inaccuracies or omissions the auditors mention them. Attention is drawn to any disagreement with the company's figures or interpretation of them. When the auditors mention any of these, their report is said to be **qualified**. Canny investors may take this as a signal to get out...fast.

Directors' Report

This statement usually goes under the title 'Board of Directors'. It gives directors' names, backgrounds, dates of appointment, and resignations if applicable. In your example of the XYZ Company, you might see that some half a dozen members of the Board are leaving as a result of a de-merger (the company being split into separate parts). Items like this can be a case where you need to ask questions: Is this a 'downsizing' exercise? Will it enable the firm to become more or less profitable? How much are the outgoing directors receiving in payoffs, if any? And do you have any qualms about the ethics?

The Profit and Loss Account

Now for a look at the financial items: the profit and loss account, balance sheet and cash flow statement. As an example, the figures for a profit and loss account shown on page 74 tell you about a XYZ's annual income/expenditure and the consequent profit or loss in the year.

Big companies usually pursue more than one type of business, and own 'subsidiary' companies. These often have their own accounts but the holding company will present consolidated profit and loss accounts. This gives the whole company's annual income and expenditure and the consequent profit or loss (P or L) in the year.

Alongside the company's results for the nine months ended 31 December 2005, is another for the year to 31 March 2005. For simplicity, only the 'continuing', not the 'discontinued' operations are shown. The reader can judge how far the company has progressed, if at all, and how much of the profit was retained in the business. From the P&L figures, the investor also learns how much of the company's profit went in tax, in dividends or other costs.

The account starts with **group turnover**, which is basically total sales of services or products. On turnover of £312m, the company made an **operating profit** of £59m which, with profits from other sources, comes to a **total operating profit** of £167m...healthy enough.

Different areas of spending are deducted from the gross profit, line by line. If insufficient funds are not allowed for depreciation of buildings, equipment and so on, the profit figures will be inflated and give a misleading picture of the company's health.

Another item that affects the gross profit is the **sale of fixed assets**. At one time, if a company sold property for more than it cost, the difference was regarded as profit. However as companies occasionally also re-valued their properties in the **balance sheet** (see page 76) this meant that they appeared to have a lot of assets, and made big profits when they sold them. Now companies have to compare the amount they get when they sell a property with its value in the balance sheet.

On **ordinary activities** the company made £68m compared with a loss in the previous year of £108m. However there is interest to pay and receive, and taxation to pay, leaving a **loss on ordinary activities after taxation** of £34m. After various other items are added and subtracted to this amount, the P&L document shows **Retained loss/profit** of £430m.

Then comes **earnings per share** (basic) of 5.5p. Earnings are calculated on profits after tax. If the tax charge falls, earnings are likely to increase faster than profits. Total earnings should more than cover the total cost of dividends on ordinary shares but in this case, as was foretold in the chairman's report, there are no dividends for the year. This shows in the nil item in the last line, **dividends per share**.

Check any divergence between earnings and profits. If, for example, a company buys a suitor with their own shares, the profits may be up, but the return on each share may be down - not a happy omen for investors. Compare the relationship between profits and sales for the current and previous years. Compare also the performance of competitors in the same period. These comparisons give a realistic idea of how well (or badly) the company is doing

Consolidated Profit And Loss Account
(Losses Are In Brackets)

	Nine months ended 31/12/05 £m	Year ended 31/03/05 £m
Turnover	790	1,021
Less: share of joint ventures' turnover	(96)	(78)
Less: share of associates' turnover	(382)	(586)
Group turnover	312	357
Operating costs, ordinary costs	(253)	(303)
Operating costs exceptional	—	(285)
Operating profit/(loss) and	59	(231)
Share of operating profit in:		
Joint ventures	14	16
Associates	94	121
Total operating profit/(loss): group and share of joint ventures and associates	167	(94)

Excluding exceptional items	167	191
Exceptional items	—	(285)
Non operating exceptional items:		
loss on operations to be discontinued	(25)	
Demerger costs	(49)	(14)
Costs of reorganisation	(25)	
Profit on disposal of fixed assets	—	
	(99)	(14)
Profit/(loss) on ordinary activities before interest	68	(108)
Interest receivable and similar income	61	
Interest payable and similar charges	(98)	
Share of interest of joint ventures and associates	(44)	
Net interest	(81)	
(Loss)/profit on ordinary activities before taxation	(13)	
Tax oil (loss)/profit on ordinary activities	(21)	
(Loss)/profit on ordinary activities after taxation	(34)	
Minority interests - equity	(4)	
(Loss)/profit for the financial period	(38)	
Ordinary dividends	—	
Demerger dividend	(392)	
Retained (loss)/profit for the financial period	(430)	
Earnings/(loss) per share:		
Basic excluding exceptional items	5.5p	
Attributable to exceptional items	(8.9)p	
Basic including exceptional items	(3.4)p	
Diluted excluding exceptional items	5.5p	
Diluted including exceptional items	(3.4)p	
Dividends per share	—	

The Balance Sheet

Everything a company owns (fixed and current assets) and owes (fixed and current liabilities) is on the balance sheet sent out at the end of the financial year. The 'balance' is the difference between them taken on a particular day, like a snapshot photo. Subsidiary accounts are merged with the group so as to report them to shareholders who get the consolidated balance sheet of the group.

In brief, the top half of the balance sheet is the net figure for what the company owns, and the bottom half is how the capital has been raised to buy it.

Shareholders rarely bother to look at the balance sheet any more than they do at the profit and loss account, and for the same reason, yet the balance sheet is a mine of information. Investors can work out whether the company is making an adequate return on capital, get an idea of its financial strength, see why the company might attract a bidder, and get an early warning sign of possible problems. The balance sheet shows the company's worth and how it is using shareholders' money.

The balance sheet values of **fixed assets** such as shops and fittings; factories or machinery or long-term investments steadily reduce over their working lives. This reduction is the counterpart of any **depreciation charge** shown in a P&L account. Companies can be overcautious or over-optimistic in their views about depreciation and the revaluation of property.

A very low depreciation charge, for example, tends to increase profits – as it is not deducted from the P&L. It may also show fixed assets as being worth more now than they actually are. But writing everything off immediately is also sometimes used to blame outgoing staff and make things look better later, a favourite ploy of newly arrived chief executives or predators who have just taken over a company.

Fixed assets are added to **current assets** (stocks, debtors, liquid investments and cash). This total is then deducted from fixed and current liabilities to give the **net assets employed**. If a company bids for another, they may pay more than the assets are worth after acquiring it and write off a portion of the price they paid for it. The excess, known as **goodwill** is cut directly from the balance sheet, not shown as a loss in the P&L. This weakens the company - especially if borrowed money has been used for the bid.

Then follow items that make up **capital and reserves**. These add up to **shareholders' funds**. With minority equity interests, these give the **total equity** of the group. This figure shows what shareholders would get (in theory) if the company stopped trading, repaid all its debts, sold off all its assets and distributed the rest to shareholders.

Cash Flow

The last part of the company accounts sent out to shareholders is the **Cash flow** statement. **Operating activities** show the net cash inflow/outflow generated by the business. **Returns on investment and finance** show interest earned and paid, from which are deducted shareholders' dividends and **tax**. **Financing activities** shows whether the company has bought or sold any fixed assets and other investments, like shares. It reveals the net position of the company. The bottom line is **increase/decrease in cash** in the period.

These areas of the cash flow reveal how much cash the business brought in, paid out and how much was re-invested in its future. Investors can see whether a company is spending cash or absorbing it rapidly. They should be wary of large cash outflows, unless there is a very good reason for them. Even then, take care that the answers do not play havoc with the truth.

Look also at **cash in the bank** and **borrowings**. If the business does not make enough money to pay off its interest, it may not survive, so check the ratio of net borrowings to shareholders' funds. This is known as the **gearing ratio**. A gearing ratio over 50 per cent is not a good sign unless there is a very adequate reason.

Summary

✔ Companies are obliged by law to produce a set of accounts. These are sent out about six weeks before the Annual General Meeting.

✔ The accounts comprise reports from auditors, directors and chairman; the **profit and loss account, balance sheet** and **cash flow statement**.

✔ If auditors **'qualify'** the accounts, the company is probably going through a financial **crisis**.

✔ The **profit and loss account (P&L)** show the company's **earnings and expenditure** and profits or loss made for the year.

✔ The **balance sheet** is a **snapshot** of all that the company owns and owes at the end of the financial year.

✔ The **cash flow** shows how much cash came into the company, was spent on dividends, tax or investment and how the remainder was used or financed.

✔ Warning signs of a business in trouble
  ● When sales are rising faster than profits
  ● Debtors are rising faster than creditors
  ● If either are rising faster than sales

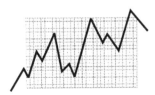

Chapter Nine

Share Valuation

KEY FEATURE:
Share Valuation techniques allow the investor to compare one share with others of a similar nature.

BECAUSE THE dividends payable on a share tend to fluctuate from year to year, and because the risks involved in holding a share are often unquantifiable, there is no exact method of finding out, in absolute terms, precisely how much an investor stands to make or lose by purchasing shares in a particular company.

There are, however, a number of share valuation techniques which investors can use to compare one share with others. These provide the investor with a rough guide to value rather than with absolute valuations. But a ball-park valuation is better than no valuation at all, so these techniques are used almost universally by professional and astute private investors alike.

There are three main techniques for evaluating a specific share, and these produce something called the **Dividend Yield, P/E Ratio** and **Net Asset Value** figures. Taking each calculation method in turn...

The Dividend Yield

The purpose of the dividend yield calculation is to help you determine how much income you are likely to receive from a particular share. There are two types of dividend yield calculation: an historic yield calculation and a prospective yield calculation.

The **historic yield** calculation is based on actual previous dividend payments. By basing the calculation on 'real' past data, an investor can determine quite accurately how much he or she stands to receive if future dividends are roughly equal in size to the ones which have already been paid.

The **prospective yield** calculation is more speculative in nature and is based on educated estimates regarding the size of future dividend payments.

Of course, neither the historic nor the prospective yield calculation can produce figures which are one hundred per cent reliable. This is because the value of a share is intrinsically linked to the value of the company which issues it. Unless you have a crystal ball and have been blessed with the gift of second sight, no one can really tell what the future has in store for any particular company. Having said that, if one assumes that past performance will be repeated - at least to some extent - in the future, the yield calculations can be extremely enlightening.

Because investors receive dividend payments after basic rate tax has been deducted, the first step in calculating the historic yield is to add this back on. To do this, use the following formula:

$$\left(\frac{\text{Net Dividend}}{\text{100-current basic rate of tax}} \right) \text{ x } 100 = \text{Gross Dividend}$$

For example, if the net dividend for a certain share was 20p, and the basic rate of tax was 20 per cent, our calculation would be:

$$(20p / (100 - 20)) \text{ x } 100$$
$$(20p / 80) \text{ x } 100$$
$$0.25p \text{ x } 100 = 25p$$

Now that you know the historic gross dividend, you can calculate how much this is as a percentage of the share. To do this, simply divide the gross dividend by the price per share and multiply by one hundred.

For example, if our 25p gross dividend was received on a share which cost £7 (700p) then the dividend yield expressed as a percentage would be:

$$25p / 700p = 0.036$$
$$0.036 \text{ x } 100 = 3.6\%$$

Calculating prospective dividend yield is even easier, because since you are simply estimating future dividends, you might as well estimate the gross dividend straight away. For example, if you know that historically a gross dividend has been around 25p per share, and the company has forecast that future dividends are expected to be fifty per cent higher, you can reasonably estimate that the gross dividend will be around 37.5p per share. Armed with that projected figure, you can then calculate how much this is as a percentage of the share itself. Again, to do this, simply divide the gross dividend by the price per share and multiply by one hundred.

For example, if the share price is still 700p, the dividend as a percentage would be:

$$37.5p / 700p = 0.054$$
$$0.054 \times 100 = 5.4\%$$

Using Dividend Yield Figures

So much for calculating dividend yield figures - how do you actually use them? Well, there are two major ways of using the figures to help you make your investment decisions, and they are:

To help balance a portfolio of shares

If your portfolio is already heavily geared to high-yield dividends which could have little potential in the way of capital growth, you may want to balance these with shares which have smaller dividend yields but which have a larger potential for future capital growth, and vice versa.

For example, if you have shares in a lot of blue chip companies, the dividend yields may be quite high, but because these companies are already well established, there is little room for potential expansion and the share price itself may not increase very much. Shares in a smaller company, although producing smaller dividends, might well have the potential to double or perhaps even triple in value over a number of years as the company expands. By balancing lower-yields with the higher ones, your portfolio should also provide a good balance between income and capital growth when viewed over the medium to long term.

To compare shares within the same market sector

If you are of the opinion that one particular market sector will do well over the next few years, you can calculate the dividend yields of the major players in this sector and decide which of them is most suited to your investment needs.

For example, if you think that the electrical retail sector is likely to experience a surge in profits, you could calculate the dividend yields for the top ten companies in this sector and then decide which share offers, in your opinion, the best potential for either income or capital growth.

It should go without saying that dividend yields should not be blindly used to help you choose shares. Basing any investment decision on pure mathematics is never to be advised. However, dividend yield figures can be a valuable aid in making investment decisions.

The Price Earnings Ratio

The Price Earnings Ratio (often called the P/E Ratio) is most commonly used when the desired outcome is a direct comparison of profits between two or more companies. It indicates the relationship between the share price and the profit potential of the company which issues it.

Before you can begin to calculate the price earnings ratio itself, you must first calculate how much of the company's earnings are available for shareholders. You do this by dividing after-tax profits by the total number of shares issued by the company.

For example, if a company has 50,000 shares in issue and profits, after the deduction of corporation tax, are £25,000, then our calculation would be:

$$£25,000 / 50,000 = 50p$$

This is the amount of money which each share has theoretically earned during the year in question. It is "theoretical" because although all earned profits belong to the shareholders, some will undoubtedly be re-invested back into the company to fund expansion, and so on.

Once you have this figure, you can calculate the price earnings ratio as follows:

Share Price / Earned profits per share = Price Earnings Ratio

If the price of the fictitious share is £3 then the calculation would be:

$$300p / 50p = 6$$

This is known as an *historic* price earnings ratio, because it is based on precise historical data (company profits after tax, share price, etc.) As with dividend yields, it is also possible to produce a *prospective* price earnings ratio, but this is vastly more complicated and relies on accurate forecasting of such data. Unfortunately, such forecasting is seldom accurate, so the prospective price earnings ratios themselves tend to be less useful than one might initially think.

Using Price Earnings Ratio Figures

P/E ratios are most commonly used when the desired outcome is a direct comparison of profits between two or more companies. Obviously for such a comparison to be made accurately, the investor must ensure that the price earnings ratio for each company is calculated over the same period.

It is also a good idea to keep Price Earnings Ratio comparisons to companies which trade in the same country and even the same business sector. This is because a comparison between two or more companies which operate in different economical climates will almost undoubtedly be more difficult to interpret.

Interpreting Price Earnings Ratios is just as much of an art (some would say more so) than it is a science. This is because no two companies are absolutely identical and this in itself will cause at least some ratio discrepancy. Large discrepancies, however, may be more significant.

Consider two companies which are very similar. One has a Price Earnings Ratio of nine and the other a ratio of 15. In this situation, the discrepancy could indicate any of the following:

- The shares of the first company are not as high as they ought to be. This would mean that they may be good value investments.

- The shares of the second company are higher than they ought to be. This would indicate that they may not be so good from an investment point of view.

- The discrepancy is caused by some factor you have not yet considered. Perhaps the companies are not as similar as you first thought.

Now obviously it is necessary to study each company in further detail before any one of these conclusions can be reached with any confidence. Using the Price Earnings Ratio has, however, given you something to focus on and is a good way of making initial, if sometimes rather crude comparisons.

Net Asset Value

One question which many prospective investors in a company want to know the answer to is this: If the bottom dropped out of the world and the company in question went into liquidation, how much might a shareholder reasonably expect to receive?

The Net Asset Value calculation is designed to answer this question. It works by dividing the total assets allocated to shares by the number of shares which have been issued (found by subtracting short- and long-term liabilities, provisions and charges from the published net asset figure).

For example, if a company has £3,000 million worth of assets allocated for ordinary shares and there are 1,500 million ordinary shares in circulation, the Net Asset Value would be:

£3,000,000,000 divided by 1,500,000,000 = £2 per share

In other words, for every ordinary share held, the shareholder could reasonably expect to receive £2 should the company cease trading. This figure can help the investor to decide if investing in a particular company is compatible with the amount of risk they are prepared to take.

For example, a low-risk investor would probably want to concentrate on companies which have higher Net Asset Value figures, whereas a more adventurous investor might be prepared to invest in companies with lower Net Asset Value figures.

Because so many investors are interested in Net Asset Value figures, many companies include them in their accounts. It may not always be necessary, therefore, to calculate the figures for yourself.

No share valuation calculation can ever be one hundred per cent accurate and they should **never** be followed blindly. Having said that, the figures provided by the calculations outlined in this chapter can often provide good **clues** as to whether or not a particular investment might be suited to your needs. Taken alongside the opinions that you form from the business press and company accounts, they can make the difference between a timely investment and missing the action.

Summary

✔ There are a number of share **valuation techniques** which investors can use to **compare** one share with others of a similar nature.

✔ The **dividend yield** calculation is designed to help you determine **how much income** you are likely to receive from a particular share.

✔ The **Price Earnings Ratio** (often called the P/E Ratio) is designed to indicate the **relationship between the price of a share and the profit potential of the company which issues it.**

✔ The **Net Asset Value** (NAV) calculation is designed to indicate **how much** a shareholder might reasonably expect to receive should the company **cease trading** and go into liquidation.

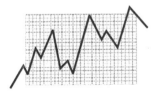

Chapter Ten

Technical Analysis

KEY FEATURE:
Technical analysis is the art of predicting whether a financial market or share price will rise or decline according to the interpretation of charted historical data.

NOW THIS MIGHT sound rather complex, but in its basic form technical analysis is really quite straightforward, and anyone with a little time can use it to help them pick probable investment winners.

There are a huge number of technical analysis indicators used by investors and many are beyond the scope of this book. Instead *Understand Shares in a Day* will limit itself to the main indicators and you will learn how to use them yourself with little more than a few sheets of graph paper, a small sample of historical share or market data and a calculator.

The Moving Average

This is the most popular technical indicator in use, and it is one which is employed by small-time private investors and

---

professional corporate investors alike. The idea is to chart a
sample of past closing prices (that is the price of a specific share
or index at the close of business each day) and then superimpose
a moving average which is the sum of previous prices divided by
the number of days used.

The idea is that when the two resulting charted lines cross, a buy
or sell signal is generated. This specific analysis method will be
described in detail in a few moments, but first you need to know
how the chart is created step-by-step. For the purposes of
example consider the share price movements of a fictitious
company called Talking Widgets Plc.

Step One - Obtain the Data

The first step is to obtain a sample of **historical data**. As indicated,
most daily newspapers have a financial page which will tell you
the closing price of the most popular shares for the previous
trading day, but if you wish to chart a more unusual share or
commodity then you may need to refer to a specialist newspaper
such as *The Financial Times* or the *Wall Street Journal*.
Alternatively, a lot of free and paid-for financial information can
be found on the Internet. Whatever medium you use to obtain
your data, the information you need is the closing price of the
share you are interested in.

The amount of data you collect will depend on what type of
investment signals you are looking for. It is generally agreed
among investment professionals that short moving averages will
give short term buy and sell signals, whilst longer moving
averages will give longer-term buy and sell signals.

For the purposes of this illustration you can construct a seven day moving average to provide short-term buy and sell signals, since the basic principle is exactly the same regardless of how much data is actually used. You therefore begin by obtaining the closing price of Talking Widgets Plc shares for the past seven days. Let's assume that they read as follows:

Day 1	360
Day 2	370
Day 3	394
Day 4	380
Day 5	385
Day 6	387
Day 7	395

Step Two - Draw a Chart

Once you have the necessary data, you can then draw up a chart so that the prices are given in diagramatical form. The date of each price should be given on the horizontal axis and the closing price should be indicated on the vertical axis. A completed chart would therefore look something like this:

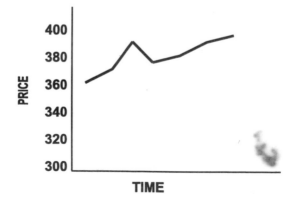

Step Three - Calculate the Moving Average

Now that you have charted the closing prices for the last seven days, you can calculate your first moving average figure. This is achieved by taking the seven closing prices and adding them together, then dividing by seven to give an average figure for the seventh day. If you add up your seven closing prices for Talking Widgets Plc, you get a figure of 2,671. Your average is therefore 2,671/7 = 381.57. The value of 381.57 is now plotted on your chart on day seven.

To find the average for subsequent days, you simply take the total of the seven previous closing prices and divide by seven. The moving average figure for day eight would therefore by the sum of days two to eight divided by seven. Day nine would be the average of days three to nine, and so on.

When an average has been calculated for the seventh day onwards, a Moving Average line will have appeared on our chart, making it look something like this:

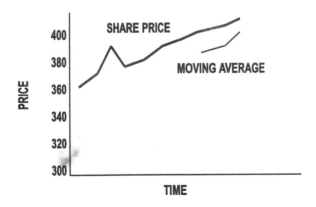

94

Now that you have a chart depicting the actual closing prices of Talking Widgets Plc and a seven day moving average line, you can begin to interpret their relationship. In brief, technical analysts believe that:

✔ If the share price line crosses the moving average line in an upward direction, a buy signal is generated.

✔ If the share price line crosses the moving average line in a downward direction, a sell signal is generated.

The Relative Strength Index

The Relative Strength Index - also known as the RSI - is a technical indicator which is believed to reveal whether a particular stock or market is overbought or oversold at any particular time. If a market is overbought then this may indicate there are too many investors holding shares. This suggests that a fall in market value will occur when some investors dump their stock in order to take profits. If a market is oversold then this may indicate there are too few investors holding shares. This suggests that more people will purchase shares and that the market will rise.

Mathematically speaking, the RSI is based on the ratio between previous price increases over previous price decreases, and can be expressed as follows:

$$RSI = 100 - 100/(1+RS)$$

where RS is the ratio of the average price gain over a period and the average price drop over the same period.

For those of you who find these types of formulae a little perplexing, this is how it is calculated, step by step...

The data you need to calculate the RSI is the *change* in closing prices of the stock or index you are dealing with. For example purposes you can use the same closing prices for Talking Widgets as you used a few minutes ago to create a seven day Relative Strength Index. Your data therefore reads something like this:

Day 1	360	+05
Day 2	370	+10
Day 3	394	+24
Day 4	380	-14
Day 5	385	+05
Day 6	387	+02
Day 7	395	+08

Now you should add together the sum total of the positive changes. These are the figures which are prefixed with an addition (+) sign. Your calculation is therefore:

$$5 + 10 + 24 + 5 + 2 + 8 = 54$$

In the same way, you now add together the sum total of the negative changes. These are the figures which are prefixed by a subtraction (-) sign. In your seven day sample there was just one negative change, so this automatically becomes your total.

$$14 + 0 = 14$$

This next step is to divide the total of positive changes by the total of negative changes, and then add one. Your calculation is therefore:

$$54 / 14 = 3.85$$
$$3.85 + 1 = 4.85$$

Now you should divide 100 by the figure we have just obtained. Your calculation here would be:

$$100 / 4.85 = 20.6$$

Finally, you subtract the figure you have just calculated from 100. This gives:

$$100 - 20.6 = 79.4$$

The Relative Strength Index figure for the seventh day is therefore 79.4. To calculate the RSI for subsequent days you simply carry out the same exercise on the data for the next batch of seven days, in much the same way as you do when calculating a moving average.

Generally speaking, technical analysts work to the following principles:

- If the RSI is above 70 then the market is thought to be overbought and a fall in share price can be expected.

- If the RSI is below 30 then the market is thought to be oversold and a rise in share price can be expected.

Some analysts use variations on these figures, such as 80 signifying overbought and 20 signifying oversold, but the principle remains the same.

The Moving Average Convergence / Divergence

Often abbreviated as the MACD, the Moving Average Convergence/Divergence technical indicator was developed by a man called Gerald Appel. It is a widely used oscillator created from the divergence between two separate moving averages - one calculated for the short term and another for the longer term.

When the underlying market is trending in one direction or the other, the shorter term moving average will rise or decline more rapidly than the longer term. The difference between the two averages is calculated and plotted on a graph as the oscillator line. As this line dips or rises above a control "zero line" so it is thought that the market may decline or rise respectively. The further the MACD oscillator moves from the zero line, the stronger the trend is thought to be.

The Price Momentum

This is defined as the ratio between the current market price of a commodity and the price of the same commodity Y days ago. The formula for calculating price momentum is very simple:

(Current value - value Y days ago) x 100

If the momentum readings are high then this implies that the commodity is overbought and that a fall may be expected.

If the momentum readings are low then this implies that the commodity is oversold and that a rise may be expected.

The Stochastic Indicator

This was developed by George Lane and is intended to measure - as a percentage - the position of a closing price in relation to the trading range of a previous time sample. Stochastics are thought be useful because they work on the premise that the closing price of a commodity is usually closer to the top of the trading range during a rising trend, but closer to the bottom of the trading range during a declining trend.

By oscillating between a range of 0 and 100, the stochastic is thought to indicate the way the trend is moving. A stochastic reading at or below 30 might suggest that a market rise is due, whilst a reading at or above 70 might suggest a market fall.

Volume Accumulation Indicator

This technical indicator was created by Marc Chaikin. It measures trading volume in relation to price fluctuations, working on the hypothesis that if a market spends most of the day on a downward trend, but ends on a positive note, the positive trend should be interpreted in relation to the whole, which was largely negative.

The Volume Accumulation Formula looks like this:

$$\text{Volume Accumulation} = \sum V \times \frac{(MC-ML)-(MH-MC)}{(MH-ML)}$$

Where MC is the Market Close, ML is the Market Low, MH is the Market High and V is the Volume.

This indicator is interpreted by comparing it with the market price and the appearance of prominent convergences and divergences are said to indicate likely changes in the market trend.

Putting Analysis to Work

If you want to start using technical analysis yourself then the best way of doing this is to begin by using both the Moving Average and the Relative Strength Index together.

By doing this you can use the RSI to confirm or reject Moving Average signals, and professional analysts believe that this improves the overall forecasting accuracy of both. The working guidelines which many successful investors use are as follows:

- If the moving average indicates that the share price or market will rise, and the relative strength index is below a value of 70, a rise in market value has been confirmed. The lower the RSI value is, the more confident you can be.

- If the moving average indicates that the share price or market will fall, and the relative strength index is above a value of 30, a fall has been confirmed. The higher the RSI value is, the more confident you can be.

- If the moving average indicates that the share price or market will rise, and the relative strength index is above a value of 70, ignore the signal. The RSI and the moving average are giving opposing advice.

- If the moving average indicates that the share price or market will fall, and the relative strength index is below a value of 30, ignore the signal. Again, the RSI and the moving average are giving opposing advice.

A Word of Caution

Whilst technical analysis is used widely throughout the investment world, it is by no means infallible. The fact is that technical analysis, as powerful and all-knowing as it can sometimes appear, is based only on past performance.

It cannot take into account budget announcements or other human factors which will affect the markets, and so has no way of predicting "shock" crashes or booms. Any such occurrences would render all of your calculations invalid. It should therefore be obvious that unless you are prepared to suffer losses when following incorrect buy or sell signals, professional advice should always be taken.

Summary

✔ **Technical analysis** is the **art of predicting** whether a financial market or share price will rise or decline according to the interpretation of historical data presented in the form of a chart.

✔ The **Moving Average** is the **most popular technical indicator** in use, and it is one which is employed by small-time private investors and professional corporate investors alike.

✔ The **Relative Strength Index** - also known as the RSI - is a technical indicator which is believed to reveal whether a particular stock or market is **overbought or oversold** at any particular time.

✔ Technical Analysis, useful as it is, cannot take into account budget announcements or other human factors which will affect the markets, and so has **no way of predicting "shock" crashes or booms**.

Chapter Eleven

Equity Options

KEY FEATURE:
Equity Options are financial products in their own right which can be used to insure the investor against falling share prices or, alternatively, to generate profits from share price fluctuations without buying the shares themselves.

TO PUT it very simply, an equity option is something which gives the investor the right - but not the obligation - to buy or sell shares at a predetermined price. There are two types of equity options, and these are:

- **Call Options** which give the investor the right to buy shares at a known price.

- **Put Options** which give the investor the right to sell shares at a known price.

Before discussing how Calls and Puts can be used by investors, there are a few fundamentals which first need to be covered...

To begin with, equity options are bought in units of one contract, and a contract gives the investor control over a certain number of shares (usually 1,000) for a limited period. The price paid for an

---

option contract is known as the **exercise price** and the date on which the contract expires is known as the **expiry date**.

The exercise price of an option depends on a number of factors, such as how long the option has to go before it expires and where the exercise price is in relation to the underlying share price. These factors are known as **time value** and **intrinsic value**.

Time Value

Obviously, the longer you have an option to buy or sell shares, the more time there is for you to generate a profit. A share has more chance of increasing or falling substantially in three months than it has in just one. Therefore, the more time value there is in an option, the higher the exercise prices for that option will be.

Intrinsic Value

This is based on the relationship between the exercise price of the option and the underlying share price. If you buy a call option which gives you the right to buy 1,000 Ocepoc shares at 550p each, and the actual share price is currently 600p, then you have 50p of positive intrinsic value. On the other hand, if the current share price was only 500p then you would have -50p of negative intrinsic value. A third possibility is that the share price is currently 550p, giving you zero intrinsic value.

● An option which has positive intrinsic value is said to be **in the money**.

● An option which has negative intrinsic value is said to be **out of the money**.

● An option which has no intrinsic value is said to be **at the money**.

What moves option prices?

Option prices move according to the type of contract and the movement of the underlying share price. If the underlying share price goes down then a call option (which gives the right to buy shares) will also go down, but a put option (which gives the right to sell shares) will go up. On the other hand, if the underlying share price goes up then a call option will go up, but a put option will go down.

For example, if Ocepoc shares are currently 600p each, the prices might be as follows:

Option		Calls			Puts		
		Jan	Apr	Jun	Jan	Apr	Jun
Ocepoc	550	50	70	80	12	20	25
(600)	600	30	50	60	30	40	45
	650	15	30	50	55	60	65

If you wanted to secure the option to buy 1,000 Ocepoc shares at 600p each until June, you would pay £600 for a Call option (60p x 1,000 shares per contract = £600). If the Ocepoc shares rose in the meantime, the option you hold would increase in value.

On the other hand, if the actual share price fell, the value of your option contract would also fall.

If you wanted to secure the option to sell 1,000 Ocepoc shares at 600p until June, you would pay £450 for a Put option (45p x 1,000 shares per contract = £450). If the Ocepoc shares fell then your option would increase in value. On the other hand, if the actual share price rose, the value of your contract would fall.

Equity options are commonly used in one of two ways. The first is to help the investor insure against falling share prices and the second is to try and generate profits from share movements without buying the shares themselves. The best way of explaining these uses is to provide examples.

Options as Insurance

Imagine that you have shares in Ocepoc plc and you want to insure against a fall in share prices. To accomplish this you could purchase a put option so that if the share falls in value, your put option increases in value. If the share rises in value then your put option would fall in value, but you can then sell this option and continue enjoying the rising shares.

By adopting this approach, what you lose on one part of the investment you gain on the other. Of course, the number of options you use will depend on the size of your share-holding, but you can see from this simple example that whether prices go up or down, your losses are minimal, if not eliminated altogether.

Options as Investments

More speculative-minded investors use options to benefit from share price rises without bothering to buy the underlying shares. For example, if an investor believes that Ocepoc shares are going to rocket in value, he can simply buy a call option at a fraction of the cost of the shares themselves. If he is right then the call option will increase in value and he can sell it at a profit. If he is wrong and the share prices fall then he can either sell his option at a loss or allow it to expire worthless.

If an investor believes that the shares of a particular company are going to plummet, he can benefit from this by buying a put option. If the shares do fall in value then his option increases in value and can be sold for a profit. If the investor is wrong and the shares rise in value, he can sell his option at a loss or allow it to expire worthless.

Although using equity options as speculative investment tools is too risky for many people, it does have a number of benefits:

● An option is almost always cheaper than the shares themselves. Just £500 can often give the investor the right to buy or sell 1,000 shares, but would seldom enable him to buy the shares. This gives the investor a lot of **leverage**, which means that he can make his money control more equity than if he bought the shares themselves.

● Options give the investor a specified risk. He knows at the outset how much he could lose in a worse case scenario if his option expires worthless.

● Potential gains are unlimited. If an investor holds a call option and the shares rise dramatically, his option will increase in value dramatically. If an investor holds a put option and the shares plummet, his option will allow him to generate great profits whilst everyone else is losing money hand over fist. It is not unknown for a successful options trader to enjoy profits which are literally thousands of times larger than his outlay.

The subject of equity options is vast to say the least, and although we will be touching on the use of options again in the next chapter, any attempt to discuss them in great detail in a book such as this would not do the subject the justice it deserves. For this reason, if you would like to study them further I highly recommend two other books in this series, *Understand Derivatives in a Day* and *Understand Financial Risk in a Day*.

Summary

✔ Equity **Options** are financial products in their own right which can be used to **insure** the investor against falling share prices or, alternatively, to **generate profits** from share price fluctuations without buying the shares themselves.

✔ A **Call option** gives the investor the **right to buy** shares at a known price.

✔ A **Put option** gives the investor the **right to sell** shares at a known price.

Chapter Twelve

Popular Investment Strategies

KEY FEATURE:
Over the past ten years, a number of investment strategies have become enormously popular with private individuals. This chapter discusses some of the most common investment strategies which you would do well to study further.

IN THIS chapter we will take a look at five popular investment strategies which are used by an increasing number of people. Before we do so, however, it is worth pointing out that no investment strategy can ever guarantee that you will make a profit every time you buy or sell shares.

No matter how much we know about the stockmarket, there will always be an element (some would say a very large element) of educated guesswork involved in predicting whether it will rise or fall, and whether individual shares will go up or down. For this reason, do not make the mistake of relying blindly on any one investment strategy. Do not invest more money than you can afford to lose should the worst happen, and always consult a professional financial advisor if you are in any doubt as to how suitable a particular strategy might be for you.

That said, let us now discuss five of the most popular investment strategies in common use today...

Cost Averaging

Commonly known as "Dollar Cost Averaging" in the USA, and "Pound Cost Averaging" in the UK, this strategy is said to work equally well regardless of whether you are investing dollars, pounds or any other currency. The basic premise behind the strategy is that investing money in shares on a regular basis is almost always more beneficial than investing "lump sums" on an irregular basis.

The theory behind this premise is quite simple. Investing on a regular basis helps to ensure that any peaks and troughs in the movement of a stock market are "averaged out" over the whole of your investment. Consider the following example:

You have $10,000 to invest in a stock which currently costs $20. If you invest all $10,000 at once you will purchase (disregarding any broker fees and commissions) 500 shares in the company.

Now the stock can do one of three things. It can go up in price, down in price, or remain the same. If it goes up $2 per month over five months, your shares would be worth $15,000 at the end of the period. If it goes down $2 per month, your shares would be worth $5,000 at the end of the period. And if the price remains the same for the five month period, your shares would remain valued at $10,000.

Compare these three scenarios with what would happen if you took your $10,000 and invested $2,000 per month for the five month period:

Rising Market

Month	Invest	Price	Shares
01	$2,000	$20	100
02	$2,000	$22	90
03	$2,000	$24	83
04	$2,000	$26	76
05	$2,000	$28	71
06	NIL	$30	——

At the end of this period in a rising market, you have invested the same $10,000 and you currently hold 420 shares. The stock value is now $30 per share. Your $10,000 investment is now worth $12,600.

Of course, if you had invested all $10,000 at $20 a share, your investment would now be worth $15,000, but you must remember that the stock market does not always go up. Let's look at how the cost averaging strategy would have worked in a falling market:

Falling Market

Month	Invest	Price	Shares
01	$2,000	$20	100
02	$2,000	$18	111
03	$2,000	$16	125
04	$2,000	$14	142
05	$2,000	$12	166
06	NIL	$10	——

Now you have invested the same $10,000, but because the stock price has been falling, you have managed to buy 644 shares. This means that your investment is now worth $6,440 compared with just $5,000 had you invested all at once.

Sideways Market

If the price of your stock remains static throughout the example period, your investment will also remain unchanged at the end of the period, as follows:

Month	Invest	Price	Shares
01	$2,000	$20	100
02	$2,000	$20	100
03	$2,000	$20	100
04	$2,000	$20	100
05	$2,000	$20	100
06	NIL	$20	——

A total of $10,000 invested is worth the same at the end of the period.

Fluctuating Market

Cost Averaging really comes into its own when it is used in the real-world environment of a fluctuating market. Consider this ten month scenario:

Month	Invest	Price	Shares
01	$2,000	$20	100
02	$2,000	$18	111
03	$2,000	$16	125

04	$2,000	$18	111
05	$2,000	$16	125
06	$2,000	$18	111
07	$2,000	$20	100
08	$2,000	$22	90
08	$2,000	$24	83
10	$2,000	$26	76

In this scenario you have invested a total of $20,000. Over the ten month period you have accumulated 1,032 shares. Each share is now worth $26, so your $20,000 investment is now worth $26,832. If you had invested all $20,000 at the outset, you would have purchased 1,000 shares, and these would now be worth $26,000. Cost Averaging has therefore helped you to generate an additional $832 over the ten month period (just over 4%).

This might not sound like a great deal to shout about, but when you consider that all the examples provided here are deliberately modest, and that cost averaging works best in volatile markets, you should be able to conclude that this strategy is well worth investigating further.

Channel Theory

Another popular strategy is based on "channel theory", which states that some stocks repeatedly "roll" between a lower "support" price and an upper "ceiling" price. Profits are generated by spotting a stock which seems to roll within a channel and then buying when it gets close to the support price and selling when it approaches its ceiling price.

For example, let's say that you have been doing your technical analysis homework and you notice something special about the chart of Success Inc. You've noticed that every few months, the stock of Success Inc. rises to around $50, then gradually falls back to $40, then starts rolling back towards $50, and so on. According to the channel theory strategy, you should think about waiting for the next fall back to $40, then buying the stock and holding it until it rises up towards $50, at which point you sell and wait for it to go back to $40. By repeating this process, the advocates of this strategy say, you can grow pretty rich, pretty quickly.

Let's take a look at how this might work in practise. Let's assume that we have found a stock which rolls regularly between $40 and $50, and that we can make one "play" each month when the stock is at $40 and that we sell when the stock hits $50. We will start with $4,000 to keep the figures nice and easy:

Month	Invest	Shares	Sell For
01	$ 4,000	100	$ 5,000
02	$ 5,000	125	$ 6,250
03	$ 6,250	156	$ 7,800
04	$ 7,800	195	$ 9,750
05	$ 9,750	243	$12,150
06	$12,150	303	$15,150

Obviously this is just an example of what might happen if you could find such a rolling stock, but it seems pretty good as far as profits are concerned. I don't know about using the strategy to "grow pretty rich, pretty quickly" but I do think that one could certainly use the strategy to help maximise profits.

Having said that, just bear in mind that few stocks "roll" forever, and sooner or later most stocks will break out of a channel - either up through the ceiling or down through the support line. As long as you are prepared for that eventuality, you aren't likely to get yourself into a position where your fingers - and dollars - get burned too badly.

Covered Calls

This strategy utilises call options which we discussed in the last chapter. As you will recall, a Call Option is a financial product which gives an individual the right, but not an obligation, to buy shares at a predetermined price.

The strategy works like this: If you have 1,000 shares in a company, you can sell someone the right, but not the obligation, to buy them from you at a predetermined price. For example, if you have 1,000 shares that cost you $40 each, you might be prepared to sell me an option to buy those shares from you for $45 each. I would pay you money for this call option - let's say $500. That $500 is yours to keep forever, but I have the legal right to purchase your shares for $45 dollars each - even if the stock rises to a price of $50 or $60. If the stock price remains lower than $45, I am unlikely to want to buy your shares for $45 each because I can get them on the open market for less. In that circumstance you get to keep the $500 I gave you for the option and you get to keep all of your 1,000 shares.

This is a great situation for you to be in. You bought the stock at $40 a share, so you won't mind selling it to me for $45 a share - especially if I'm willing to pay you $500 just for the option of doing so. If your stock goes down in value, you keep my $500 and I'm very unlikely to buy your stock at $45 a share. But even if your stock goes up in value, you make $5 a share and you get to keep my $500 option fee.

Of course, there is one possible downside to covered calls, and that is if your $40 shares rise in value to maybe $50 or $60. In that case you still have to sell me your shares for $45. In other words, you may make less from offering the covered call than you would if you sold your shares on the open market.

The up-side however, is that even if the stock rockets, you will still be $500 better off for having sold me the option. If the stock soars to $90, you will still have made $500 on my option fee and $5 profit per share. In other words, writing the covered call has enabled you to reduce your potential losses by $500 and guarantee a minimum profit of $5 per share should you get "called out" (this is where the option purchaser exercises his option and buys your shares at the predetermined price.)

Covered call writing is becoming increasingly popular as more and more investors begin to realise that this strategy could help them to make or save money whichever way the market moves. Indeed, some investors seem to focus entirely on writing covered calls, such is their enthusiasm for this strategy.

Stock Splits

The fourth investment strategy we will discuss concerns stock splits. A stock split is something that often happens when the price of a share in an individual stock rises to the point where it appears "too expensive" for the masses. When that happens, the company issuing the stock can decide to "split" it two or more ways, thus reducing the price of the stock by at least half.

For example, if shares in a company cost $100 each, the issuing company may declare a "two for one split". This means that if you hold ten $100 shares, you will now instead hold twenty $50 shares. A "four for one split" would mean that you now hold forty $25 shares, and so on.

That's the technical side of a stock-split, but what does it have to do with being an investment strategy? Well, if you look at many companies which have stock splits, you will notice that often the price of each share after the split starts climbing. For example, if our $100 share is split into two $50 shares, in many cases it will quickly climb to $60 or more. The reason for this is hard to pin down, but is probably something to do with mass psychology and the fact that the shares are now much more affordable. Anyone who has watched the stock intermittently will see the $50 tag and remember that the stock used to trade at $100, so they will buy thinking the stock is 'now' cheap. Whatever the reason, people start buying - sometimes en masse - and the share price starts climbing again.

The investment strategy involved here should now be pretty easy to figure out. Investors wait for a stock split announcement and then do one of two things:

● Buy the stock before it splits and hold onto the shares. The shares will then split and - hopefully - the price of them will start climbing. The newly split shares are then sold and a good profit taken.

● Buy call options in the stock as soon as it splits. This gives you the right, but not the obligation, to buy the shares at an agreed price. If a $100 share splits into two $50 shares, you might buy a call option to buy 1,000 shares at $55 each. If the shares then climb to $60, you can either exercise the option (buy 1,000 shares at $55 each) or sell your call option at a profit.

It has to be said that share prices do not always rise after a stock split, but in some cases the post-split rise is said to be as reliable as clockwork. This makes the Stock Split investment strategy well worth investigating further.

Bottom Fishing

The last of our five popular investment strategies is called Bottom Fishing. In a nutshell, it involves waiting for a lull in the stock market and then looking for shares in companies which seem to be priced lower than they are truly worth.

You will recall from our discussion in an earlier chapter that mass psychology often comes into play in the rises and falls of a stock market. This mass psychology is very often based on emotion rather than logic. If a stock market correction is in progress, many thousands of investors may start dumping stock without even thinking of how valuable that stock is. Because of this, it is often possible to buy shares in dull markets for a fraction of what they were worth a month or two previously.

The bottom fisher specialises in buying these shares and then holding them until the market rises and the share price follows suit. When the market stabilises and the share price has increased, the bottom fisher usually sells his holding at a profit and waits for the markets to get depressed at some point in the future.

Bottom fishing is an interesting strategy because it calls for the investor to keep his head whilst all around are losing theirs. Instead of panicking about stock market crashes and corrections, the bottom fisher takes advantage of the mass paranoia and aims to capitalise on the situation.

Obviously, your success or failure as a bottom fisher depends on your ability to spot a truly under-valued share, but once again this is a strategy which the more astute among you should investigate further.

A Word to the Enthusiastic

If, after reading this chapter, you find yourself with dollar signs in your eyes and dreams of infinite wealth in your mind, take a step back for a moment. Your enthusiasm is to be applauded, but don't let it blind you to the obvious down-side of stock market investment. No matter how reliable a strategy has been throughout history, there is always the chance that it will fail at some point in the future. After all, if any one strategy could guarantee success, we would all be millionaires already and you wouldn't be reading this book.

Approaching investment strategies with a realistic head on your shoulders is much more likely to help you invest more effectively. Give thought to the fundamentals of the companies you invest in, and perhaps make it a rule only to invest in companies you are confident in. This approach will help to ensure that if you do happen to get stuck with a few thousand shares for longer than you originally anticipated, you won't be too disappointed.

Summary

✔ **Cost Averaging** is a strategy which involves investing **smaller amounts** on a **regular basis**, rather than large amounts infrequently.

✔ The **Channel Theory** strategy involves identifying a stock which **"rolls" between a lower and an upper price** and then routinely buying at the lower price with a view to selling at the higher price.

✔ **Covered Calls** enable the investor to sell an individual the right, but not the obligation, to purchase his shares at a predetermined price.

✔ The **Stock Split** strategy involves **identifying a stock which is about to split** and then investing in it - either before the split by purchasing the stock itself, or as soon as the split has occurred by purchasing a call option.

✔ **Bottom Fishing** is the strategy of **purchasing shares at below their true value** during market corrections and lulls, with a view to selling these at a profit when the market recovers.

Chapter Thirteen

Computer Aided Investment

KEY FEATURE:
The personal computer has enormous processing power and can complete complex mathematical problems in the blink of an eye. For this reason, many private investors are using computer technology to try and increase their success at the stock market game.

HAVING DISCUSSED the topics of technical analysis and popular investment strategies, you may well be wondering how on earth anyone could ever have the time to keep track of share prices, calculate moving averages and think about stock splits, writing covered calls or profiting from the channel theory strategy. After all, most of us have day jobs or other commitments which we must attend to, don't we? Does this mean that profiting from shares is reserved only for those who have nothing else to do?

Maybe twenty years ago such a conclusion would have been accurate. Back then, private investors had to draw charts the hard way - with a pad and pencil - and the only help they had was the humble pocket calculator. These days however, things are different. The personal computer and the Internet have brought active personal investment within the reach of anyone who truly wants to get involved.

Although many prospective investors are sceptical about relying on technology to help them take care of their money, a personal computer, or PC, can be the best friend you will ever have in the world of share investment. Not only can it perform pages of advanced arithmetical calculations within a fraction of a second, it can also help you to keep track of share prices and - perhaps even more importantly - help you identify possible buy and sell signals generated by its automated technical analysis capabilities.

In short, a modern personal computer can be likened to a personal financial assistant who is on call twenty-four hours a day, seven days a week, to provide you with all the up-to-the-minute information you need to succeed as a private investor.

In this chapter we will look at all aspects of computer aided investing, from the hardware and software most commonly used through to a discussion of data feeds and on-line trading. Let us begin then, by first of all talking about...

The Personal Computer

A modern personal computer can be divided into six separate components for the purposes of discussion. These are:

Central Processing Unit (CPU)

The CPU is the "brain" of a personal computer, since it is responsible for processing all of the information it receives. The effectiveness of the CPU is generally gauged by the speed at which it operates, measured in Megahertz (MHz) or Gigahertz (GHz). A computer which operates at 1.5GHz will therefore be less effective than one which operates at 2GHz.

The Hard Disk

The hard disk is where the computer can permanently store information for future reference. Again, the larger the hard disk in terms of capacity, the better it is for the user. Hard disk capacity, like Random Access Memory, is measured in megabytes and gigabytes.

Random Access Memory (RAM)

The RAM is the "short-term memory" of a personal computer. The more RAM a computer has, the more easily and efficiently it will be able to deal with the information it manages. RAM is measured in Kilobytes (K), Megabytes (Mb) and Gigabytes (Gb). For the record, one kilobyte of memory can hold 1,024 bytes of information, one megabyte is equal to 1,024K and one Gigabyte is equal to 1,024Mb.

When personal computers were first introduced to the general public, Bill Gates, founder of Microsoft, commented that "640K of memory should be enough for anyone." Whilst this may have been true at the time, computer technology has advanced rapidly since the early days and today you won't find many machines for sale with less than 128Mb of RAM as standard. Indeed, by the time you read this, 256Mb or even 512Mb is likely to be the standard amount of RAM offered on a machine.

CD or DVD Drive

A CD or DVD drive allows the computer to read information which has been stored on special Compact Discs or Digital Versatile Disks. The efficiency of a CD or DVD drive is gauged by its speed. A few years ago an eight-speed CD ROM drive was top-of-the range, but today a similarly high-spec machine would boast a 48-speed drive, a rewriteable CD or a DVD player.

The Monitor

The monitor is the television-type screen which displays the output of the computer for the user. Monitors can be monochrome, but more commonly these days they are capable of displaying full colour images. This is one part of the computer where size is relatively unimportant. Although large screen monitors are available, the vast majority of PC owners are satisfied with a standard twelve or fourteen inch model.

The Modem

A modem (modulator-demodulator) allows a computer to connect to the Internet and exchange information with other computers using the telephone line. Its effectiveness is measured in bits per second (bps) and the more bits of information it can handle each second, the better.

Modems with speeds of 14,400bps or 28,800 bps used to be the most common, but once again, technology is advancing all the time, and at the time of going to press 56K modems are the most popular. However, broadband services, which can download 4Mb of data in under 30 seconds and are 'always on', are hitting the streets. Although relatively expensive, you will immediately see the possible benefits of having a permanent connection to share price updates.

Now although the actual components themselves (CPU, RAM, hard disk, CD ROM drive, monitor and modem) will probably remain pretty much the same for the foreseeable future, all of the above information is subject to change as far as speeds, efficiency and capabilities are concerned.

Obviously, as technology continues to advance and becomes cheaper to produce, CPUs, CD/DVD drives and modems will operate faster whilst RAM and hard disks will get bigger. The rule of thumb to use when buying a personal computer is therefore to buy as much power you can afford - but don't let numbers go to your head. Just because a new machine with a faster CPU and more RAM becomes available doesn't mean that your old one is now defunct. The fact is that a good PC can serve you well long after it has gone out of "style".

Software

Once you have a computer, you will need some software. This comes in all shapes and sizes and is readily available through PC magazines or from computer stores. But before you rush out to buy a software title, you first need to spend some time thinking carefully about how you want your computer to help you as a private investor.

Here are just some of the ways in which your PC can help you. Select whatever options seem most appropriate to you and then make sure that any software you purchase can meet your needs in full. This will prevent you from buying a costly product, which you may never fully benefit from.

General Financial Organisation

This is simply the organisation and tracking of your personal or small business finances. You begin by telling your PC how much you have in your bank accounts, or on your credit cards, and then every time you spend or receive money, you record the transaction on the computer. Your PC then updates all of your balances accordingly so that you always know what your bottom line is.

This is the most basic way in which your PC can help you with your finances, and the need is catered for by packages such as Microsoft Money and Intuit's Quicken.

Share Price Tracking

Of more specific interest to private share investors is share price tracking. This is where your PC takes share prices and records them for future reference. The data can be shown in the form of a stock chart and some packages will also enable you to use some simple technical analysis tools such as moving averages, stochastics and so on.

Almost any spreadsheet (such as Microsoft's Excel) will help you to keep track of your shares. So if you already have such a package and all you want is to track a handful of stock market prices, you may well find that you already have all you need as far as this is concerned.

Internet Data Retrieval

You can use your PC to download share price data from the Internet. All you need is a suitable connection to the Internet and a reliable information source. You'll be able to find share price information by simply clicking through from financial press sites or performing a search on a search engine such as Google. However, if you'd like recommendations on specific sites, please see *Investing on the Internet*, by Scott Western and also published by TTL.

The most reliable data on the Internet is not, in my opinion, free. The most reliable companies which allow you to download their information charge a small monthly or annual fee for the privilege. Of course, how much you are prepared to pay depends on how valuable the information is to you and how valuable your time is, but don't expect a totally free ride as far as reliable and prompt data is concerned.

Technical Analysis

Because computers can process masses of mathematical information in a matter of seconds, they are ideal for the application of technical analysis tools. At the click of a button, your PC can produce moving averages, relative strength indicators, over-bought and over-sold signals and much, much more.

This facility will save you a lot of time in calculating moving averages, etc., using just a calculator. Even better, because personal computers are dab-hands at math, you can virtually guarantee that any technical analysis indicators used will be accurate to the nth degree.

Spreadsheets are capable of producing technical analysis indicators as long as you know how to implement the formulae, but if you intend to use technical analysis on a regular basis you would be better served by investing in a stand-alone package which is designed specifically for this purpose.

Automatic Signal Generation

Finally, your PC has the power to do the ultimate as far as share investment is concerned: it can automatically retrieve and analyse share data, then signal you every time it comes across what it considers to be a buy or sell signal.

To enjoy the luxury of such automation, you will need to invest in a whistles-and-bells software package which can routinely download information from the Internet and perform technical analysis on your behalf. Another alternative is to sign up to one of the numerous websites that will alert you when your pre-set conditions (say a particular share price) are met. These can be expensive, but if you are serious about becoming a successful private investor then the expense involved in acquiring such software will be more than justified by the time you save and the signals it generates.

Of course, you don't have to act every time the computer finds a buy or sell signal, but it's good to know that you won't miss a trading opportunity just because you didn't have time to manually look at every chart for every stock you track on your PC.

Online Dealing

See chapter 14.

Mobile Computing

Having discussed the use of personal computers, let us briefly turn our attention to what seems to be a most exciting development in computer technology - the advent and evolution of the mobile Internet.

Mobile phones or Personal Digital Assistants (PDAs) can now connect to the Internet. This allows you to retrieve data whilst on the move. Even if you are sitting by the pool on your vacation, you can still download your usual share price data, analyse the information and then, if you decide that it is time to buy or sell some shares, use your mobile to place a buy or sell order with your broker. Thus, you have a great opportunity to generate stock market profits without sacrificing any of your tanning hours.

If you don't think that mobile computing is something you need right now then you are probably right, but don't write the whole subject off just yet. If you begin using a normal desktop personal computer to help you make your share investment decisions and this proves to be successful, it won't be long before you start thinking seriously about investing whilst on the move. And who knows - in ten years time PDAs may be all there is.

Summary

✔ Personal computers can help the share investor in many ways. They can crunch numbers, carry out technical analysis and even provide buy and sell signals for you to investigate further.

✔ To get the most out of a personal computer, you need to buy software that is most suited to your needs. There is a wide range of PC software for the share investor to choose from, so know what you want from a package before you buy.

✔ Mobile computing is becoming increasingly popular, and many experts predict that laptop, notebook and palmtop computers will eventually be just as popular as their desktop counterparts.

✔ A personal computer will not make you an automatic stock market whiz, but it can be an invaluable aid for the serious investor when used in conjunction with your own knowledge and common sense.

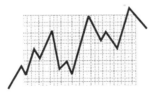

Chapter Fourteen

Dealing Online

KEY FEATURE:
Buying and selling your shares over the Internet can dramatically decrease your costs.

ONLINE INVESTMENT has grown rapidly over the years, fuelled unfortunately by the popularity of technology stocks (which after an initial glow of success, then failed to perform.) In the last three months of 1999, Internet based deals rose over 140 per cent. So what are the advantages and disadvantages of this type of execution? And how do you start?

In spite of the increase in online share dealing, this type of transaction accounts for only a minority of all share trades. More people will undoubtedly go online in the future, but for the time being at least, most investors still prefer to deal by phone. They find buying or selling shares in this way is uncomplicated. They get any share perks around; their shares come in certificate form which provides proof of ownership and allows them to deal with any broker that they choose or change a broker without delay or fuss. No money has to be paid upfront before dealing begins. The tried and tested system of phoning with calls recorded, is, save for the occasional mishap, reasonably safe.

The big disadvantage of phone dealing, however, is in the time it takes to process a deal. After waiting for what seems an eternity, and forced meanwhile to listen to the torture of an interminable opera (probably Wagnerian), investors become as frustrated as the publisher who could not understand why Marcel Proust took eight pages to describe a man turning over in bed. The share price, particularly of volatile stocks, meanwhile zigs and zags so much that dealing becomes too risky even for the high roller, let alone the fearful beginner. What is more, it is when you really need to deal that the phone lines are busiest, because everyone else is beating you to it.

But online dealing has disadvantages, too. Investors receive confirmation of their holdings in electronic form, not in the 'comfort' and proof of ownership of a tangible share certificate. Their shares are in the name of a nominee account, so cannot easily be sold through another broker, and they get no shareholder perks that might be on offer. The biggest disadvantage of all is that money has to be paid upfront before any dealing can begin. The other side of this situation is that when you sell a share, you do not have to wait for the cash. It goes immediately into the account, which has been opened for you by the broker and the bank.

Any disadvantages of online dealing are outweighed however, by their advantages. Transactions are quick, cheap and efficient. Unless a hacker breaks in, or the investor forgets or loses his or her PIN number or password, it is arguably safer than phone/post trading. The bank account set up when trading begins, records all dividends, interest and other money paid in or out (and might, at a stretch, be useful if the investor is being pursued by a fractious

spouse, investigative solicitor, aggressive creditor or an officer of
the Inland Revenue).

Tax calculations are simplified by the excellent system of record
keeping. For the richer, older investor, this helps with any
allocation of gifts or other transactions made for the purpose of
reducing their tax liabilities.

Back to Basics

Going online enables you to see the current prices of your shares
at a glance, how much they have gone up or down since their
purchase, the total value of your portfolio and what percentage it
has risen or fallen since its inception. But before this happy
Elysium of pick and tick is reached, you must, as stated at the
beginning of this section, have the basics.

They comprise computer, modem, and phone line and an Internet
service provider (see Chapter 13). Instead of a computer, the
really IT literate can get online by a digital TV, games console,
mobile phone or a dedicated email phone. With these basics, you
will be able to instruct an online broker from the shores of Loch
Lomond or a hideout in the West Indies.

To trade online, you need brokers' names, their range of services
and commission rates. Then you can set off on the mechanics of
dealing. Brokers' names and websites are listed in the financial
columns of newspapers and financial magazines. You can also
find this data by using search engines such as Alta Vista,
Askjeeves, Excite, Lycos, Yahoo, etc.

You will probably decide to go for one of the 'cheaper' brokers. But, please take care. Brokers vary in the amount of extra information such as prices, news and other background that they give. Charges may also vary depending on the number of trades you make, and the sizes of those deals. Some brokers have a sliding scale, others a flat rate.

It is very difficult to compare online brokers' directly because of the different charging structures: percentage cost, minimum and maximum cost or special offers. Some brokers now offer to online investors, special rates for frequent trades, chequebooks, interest bearing accounts, newsletters, bulletin boards, free research and 'tip sheets'. Even with these 'extras', however, the cost of two lots of commission for buying and selling, plus stamp duty on purchases, often seems disproportionate for those who are dealing only in small amounts.

If you have the time and patience and a good idea of the amount and frequency of your dealing pattern, you should be able to cut your dealing charges dramatically.

The Next Step

Bearing these facts in mind, you finally choose your broker. On the computer screen will come up a registration form. Complete this including an acceptance of the 'disclaimer' (protection against money laundering), print out the page and send it to the chosen broker with your cheque. You will receive a nominee bank account, password and PIN number. After that and providing your cheque has been cleared, registration is immediate; you can start trading. Later, by post, will come a 'welcome' letter and your new chequebook.

Your own payment cheque for your shares is essential because, unlike dealing by phone, where you pay after your deal, in online transactions you must have money in your online account before you buy a share. A fee is often charged for the administration of the account, including the banking element. However, money deposited in the bank gets a higher rate of interest than an ordinary deposit account.

When you want to trade, log in, fill in your user name and password both of which are given to you when your account is opened. Complete with the name or code of the share you want to buy/sell, and state if you wish, a price limit. You may be told that this price is not possible. An alternative quote will be given. Decide whether you want to deal at this price or not and press the appropriate button. As a new customer, you pay for the first trade by cheque but later deals are charged by direct debit from the bank account set up for you.

Lower Charges Overseas

Perhaps the main advantage of online dealing is the lower dealing costs. Phone trades can cost, in commission, one per cent up to £3,500 and 0.1% above, with a minimum of £15. Add on 0.5% Government stamp duty and these charges soon make a dent in a small profit.

However, deals through US online brokers are much cheaper and you are offered a wider range of shares than in the UK, plus full information on them, a 60 seconds execution speed and no stamp duty to pay (UK citizens must sign a certificate of foreign status of beneficial owner for United States Tax Witholding, form W-8BEN).

As an example, you use the phone to buy 544 Pearson shares at a total cost of £9,983.76. You will pay commission of £41.50 and stamp duty of £49.92. If you assume a similar £40 commission when you want to sell the shares, then the share price must rise by around 25p just to break even on the overall deal.

Online buying of the shares through the same broker, (not the cheapest), costs only £25 commission plus stamp duty and around the same price of £25 to sell, depending on the share price.

By contrast, commission for a similar transaction in the US for two deals at $9.99 each is $19.98 or £12-£14 depending on the exchange rate, with no stamp duty payable. Even the cheapest UK commission cannot get close to matching US dealing prices.

The big danger however for share dealing outside the UK and one that will become more important in the not too distant future, is the currency risk. Anybody who bought shares in a German blue chip stock at the right time and held them for two years, could have made a 35% gain and seen it all dribble away by the fall in the euro. To avoid this scenario with the dollar, it is better to deal in small sums. Cheap costs create larger profits. Set a stop loss of 5%-15%, varying with your aversion to risk, and before you leap across the Atlantic (or the Channel) in search of the Golden Fleece, make sure the landing is soft.

Summary

Phone or online? Go for the system with which you are most comfortable.

Phone dealing suits people who
- Have lots of patience and are not hard of hearing
- Are in for the long haul and prepared to wait for a good opportunity to buy or sell
- Like their shares in paper form
- Feel that phone dealing is safer and more private than an online account
- Want to deal through and change brokers without restrictions
- Prefer to pay for shares from their own bank accounts and do not mind waiting for cash after selling their shares
- Like to attend Annual General Meetings to mingle with the Board, express their feelings about the management or for a congenial cup of tea and biscuits, when available.

Online dealing suits people who
- Are IT literate or can quickly become so
- Know what shares they want and need no advice other than that which they can get from web sites
- Have some spare cash to start with and leave in their account
- Want a quickly available record of their share transactions, including dividends received, current value of their portfolio and real time share prices
- Do not mind the restriction of having only one broker
- Want a speedy efficient dealing service

Conclusion

So there you have it - a whistle-stop tour of the world of share investment. As I said at the beginning of this book, my aim has been to explain in simple terms exactly what shares are, how they work in relation to the stock market and how anyone can begin profiting from them as safely as possible.

You should now have enough knowledge to make an informed decision as to whether or not shares can help you to achieve your investment goals. If you think they can then the next step is for you to start studying the subject in more detail. If you have decided that shares are not for you, then at least this book will have saved you a lot of time and trouble.

For me, the stock market is like nothing else on earth. In my opinion, it is more than a casino environment where bets are placed. It is a microcosm of the world economy which gives us all the opportunity to invest in the companies which make a difference and help to build the shape of the future.

I hope that in this book you have come to understand that the world of shares is not as complicated as many people think. As you have seen, even professional forecasting techniques such as technical analysis can be adopted by the private investor. If this helps you to achieve professional profits then so much the better.

BEST WISHES

Glossary

Bear
Someone who is of the opinion that the stock market will fall.

Bear Market
An underlying downward stock market trend.

Bearer Shares
These belong to the person who holds the share certificate. No register of share-holders is kept as far as bearer shares are concerned.

Bid
The price at which shares are sold.

Bottom Fishing
The strategy of purchasing shares at below their true value during market corrections and lulls, with a view to selling these at a profit when the market recovers.

Broker
A person who buys and sells shares on behalf of his clients.

Bull
Someone who is of the opinion that the stock market will rise.

Bull Market
An underlying upward stock market trend.

Capital Gain
The profit realised on an investment or asset when it is sold.

Capital Loss
A loss realised on an investment or asset when it is sold.

Channel Theory
A strategy which involves identifying a stock which "rolls" between a lower and an upper price and then routinely buying at the lower price with a view to selling at the higher price.

Convertible Preference Shares
These can be converted to ordinary shares on specific dates at predetermined rates.

Cost Averaging
A strategy which involves investing smaller amounts on a regular basis, rather than large amounts infrequently.

Cum-Dividend
A security or share which allows the investor to receive all of the interest which has accrued since the last official dividend payment date.

Cumulative Preference Shares
These are Preference Shares which give the share-holder the ability to claim any unpaid dividends at a later date.

Deferred Shares
These do not normally qualify for dividends until a predetermined date or profit level has been reached.

Dividend
A share of profits paid to a share-holder.

Equity Options
Financial products which give the investor the right - but not the obligation - to buy or sell shares at a predetermined price.

Ex-Dividend
A security or share which does not allow the investor to receive any interest which is due on the next official dividend payment date.

Exercise Price
The price paid for an option contract.

Expiry Date
The date on which an option contract expires.

Inflation
A reduction in the purchasing power of money due to a sustained increase in the Retail Price Index.

NAV
The Net Asset Value of a company.

Offer
The price at which shares are bought.

Option
See Equity Option.

Ordinary Share
The most common type of shares in the modern market, giving the share-holder the right to vote at share-holder meetings.

P/E Ratio
The Price Earnings Ratio of a company.

Penny Share
A Penny Share has a low price in relation to the broader market.

Preference Shares
These give the share-holder preference over ordinary share-holders in the list of payments to creditors.

Redeemable Preference Shares
These are more like loans than true shares, because they have fixed repayment dates.

Share
A share in the financial future of a company.

Shareholder
A person who owns one or more shares.

Spread
The difference between the Bid and the Offer, also known as the Bid-Offer Spread.

Stock Split Strategy
This strategy involves identifying a stock which is about to split and then investing in it - either before the split by purchasing the stock itself, or as soon as the split has occurred by purchasing a call option.

Technical Analysis
The art of predicting whether a financial market or share price will rise or decline according to the interpretation of historical data presented in the form of a chart.